Roderick Henry Smith

The Science of Business

A Study of the Principles Controlling the Laws of Exchange

Roderick Henry Smith

The Science of Business
A Study of the Principles Controlling the Laws of Exchange

ISBN/EAN: 9783337121587

Printed in Europe, USA, Canada, Australia, Japan

Cover: Foto ©Suzi / pixelio.de

More available books at **www.hansebooks.com**

THE

SCIENCE OF BUSINESS

A STUDY OF THE

PRINCIPLES CONTROLLING THE
LAWS OF EXCHANGE

BY

RODERICK H. SMITH

NEW YORK & LONDON
G. P. PUTNAM'S SONS
The Knickerbocker Press
1888

PREFACE.

THE record of facts included in the following chapters was not originally compiled for publication, but rather to satisfy the spirit of personal inquiry. As new facts, however, came to light and arranged themselves alongside those already acquired, a body of truth was formed, which in the opinion of the writer, merited the name that this book bears, and which has induced him to submit his investigations to the public.

In order to facilitate the explanation of the facts afforded by the statistics of business, it was necessary that some guiding principles should be kept in sight, and to establish these principles the two chapters included in Part First were written. The laws there briefly considered, the Direction of Motion, and the Rhythm of Motion, have received universal acceptance from scientific men, and are great aids to help us to understand the phenomena of business.

As this work is intended for the use of business men, it has been my object to condense, as much as was possible, the treatment of the topics considered in the different chapters, and this has detracted somewhat from any literary style the work may have, by necessitating in many cases, and sometimes without notice, a quick change in the subject-matter. This fault is, however, not greatly to be regretted as it has been my endeavor to ascertain the truth, rather than to achieve artistic merit.

Thanks are due to Messrs. R. G. DUN & Co. for information concerning failures; also to Messrs. WM. B. DANA & Co., publishers of the *New York Commercial and Financial Chronicle*, for permission to use their excellent review of the New York Stock Market, and to the AMERICAN IRON AND STEEL ASSOCIATION, of Philadelphia, for information relative to the iron industry.

DUNKIRK, N. Y., July, 1885.

TABLE OF CONTENTS.

Part First.

CHAPTER PAGE
I. The Direction of Motion 1
II. The Rhythm of Motion 10

Part Second.

I. General Business 23
II. Iron 42
III. Railroad Building and Consumption of Rails 54
IV. Immigration 62
V. Stocks 67
VI. Exchange 110
VII. Foreign Trade 125
VIII. Grain 132
IX. The Balancing of Prices or Equilibration 145
X. Summary and Conclusion 162

THE SCIENCE OF BUSINESS.

PART I.

CHAPTER I.

THE DIRECTION OF MOTION.

NATURE, when viewed from an intellectual standpoint, presents to our minds the display of forces, countless in number, varied in aspect, and intricate in operation; forces that control the motions of the planets and the stars, that, upon our own earth, have caused forests to grow in the carboniferous age, and formed the coal beds which propel the machinery of the nineteenth century; forces which clear forests and found cities; forces which plant harvests and reap them; forces which establish governments and make a language, a literature, a society.

Throughout this great conflict, there are certain laws which hold true concerning all phenomena, two of which, the Law of the Direction of Motion and the Law of Rhythm, will respectively form the subject-matter of this and the following chapter.

The Law of the Direction of Motion, as formulated by Mr. Spencer, is as follows:

Motion takes the line of least resistance or of the greatest traction, or of their resultant.

Illustrations of this law are numerous. Instance the fall of the stone to the earth, when dropped from the hand, as motion in the line of greatest traction; and a feather, when dropped from the same distance, as an illustration of the resultant line of resistance — the forces at work being the attraction of gravity and the resistance of the atmosphere; the path of the falling feather being deflected from a straight line because of its greater resistance to the air.

The balloon, whose bulk is lighter than the same bulk of surrounding air, rises, and its direction from moment to moment is the line of resultant resistance determined by the relation between the attraction of the earth, the amount of gas contained, the weight of the ballast, and the force and direction of the wind.

The sun shining upon the bosom of a lake heats the air and makes it capable of absorbing moisture, and this air, being warmer and lighter than the surrounding atmosphere, rises till its upward motion is stopped when its volume is of equal weight with an equal volume of air about it. The moisture-laden cloud, being transferred by winds to a cool mountain side, or into a colder region, condenses and deposits its vapor in rain, which, as is commonly observed, falls at a tangent to the horizon. The rivulet to which the rain gives its supply of water runs in the lowest valleys, falls over the rocks, whirls around in eddies, and bends its way through the softest soils, till it reaches the ocean; the water throughout its course, whether in shape of vapor, mist, rain, snow, or river, having always and everywhere followed the line of least resistance, or of greatest traction, or of their resultant.

The fact, as noted by the United States Signal Service, that storms move out of regions of high barometric pressure into regions of low barometric pressure, is one of like significance, and, knowing the barometric pressure at different points, it is possible to predict, with the aid of the law of which we are speaking, the direction and velocity which the far-off storm will take; and, were all the factors which constitute the phenomena of storms known and measurable, it would be possible to predict, not hours but days in advance, their birth, duration, and direction. Toward such a goal the youthful science of Meteorology is progressing.

When the Jeannette was imbedded in floating ice north of Behring Strait, it was predicted, by one of the crew that her course would be northwest, or the resultant line between the known current, which set strongly to the north, and the prevailing easterly winds. Subsequent events proved the wisdom of the prediction.

The ocean currents, while seeming, at first, exceptions to the law, are, when closely examined, found to be apt confirmations of it. Their general course is away from the equator and towards the poles. This is explicable from the fact that the large amount of vapor which the sun raises in the heated regions causes a partial vacuum, which the cold water from the north, keeping close to the bottom of the sea on account of its greater weight, rushes in to fill; while the warm surface water flows off towards the poles, to fill the void left by the retreating cold currents.

That this is a true explanation of the process has recently received additional confirmation by lowering a self-registering thermometer at the equator to a great depth, when it was found that the temperature of the water was the same as in the polar regions; thus proving that there must be submarine cold currents which set toward the equator, as we know there are warm surface currents which flow away from it.

Chemistry will furnish us with another example in the familiar reaction by which hydrogen gas is produced by placing sulphuric acid and zinc together; the zinc uniting with the sulphur and oxygen in the acid, and driving off the hydrogen, which can only be explained by saying that zinc has a greater affinity or force for the sulphur and oxygen than has the hydrogen, which, as it must give up to the greater force, it is obliged to leave. The affinities of the elements are of course of different strength, but wherever we see a reaction between elements we may be sure that that reaction will take the line of greatest force. That, in the formation of snowflakes and ice crystals, the frozen water arranges itself along lines of least resistance, all will probably agree, and the crystalline forms of quartz and minerals are products in whose shapes we see additional confirmation of the law.

Among geological phenomena also we can see evidence that motion has followed the line of least resistance.

From the evidences in the earth's crust we are obliged to think of a far-distant time when the globe rolled through the heavens a molten mass; and when the water, now in the oceans, was suspended as vapor in the atmosphere. In the cooling process, which was and is now going on, there came a time when the temperature of the external earth was below 212 degrees, which would allow the vapor to be deposited, thus contracting the volume of the earth.

At a subsequent period, owing to further cooling and contraction, the mountain chains and continents appeared on the lines of least resistance. That continents so formed have been modified by subsequent events, such as eruptions, elevations and subsidences, land-slides, glaciers, rivers, lakes, and the action of the weather in the line of greatest traction or least resistance, or their resultant, is included in the description of each phenomenon.[1]

The history of the past teaches us that civilization moves along lines of least resistance. Among savage tribes the most powerful will drive the weaker tribes before them, and, in localities — as near the sea — where food is plentiful and means of communication between each other

---

[1] It may be objected that the principles we are endeavoring to establish are self-evident propositions; and that statement of them is sufficient for conviction; and it is replied that general laws have very little weight with most minds until it is shown how and why the generalization has been made.

and strange tribes is made easy, will increase in numbers and civilization. Instead of each man making his own weapons of war, those who possess the greatest aptitude for making weapons will make them; those who best can till the ground, do so, and exchange their products for weapons. Thus arise different branches of industry, and a commerce. Market days are held where different commodities are exchanged, and as the population becomes larger, and the commodities of exchange increase in number and value, necessity will arise, between buyer and seller, for laws regulating such interchange. Thus a nation is born, which increases in wealth and power in proportion as the people of which it is composed increase in the variety and extent of their commercial relations. Between tribes, also, the "logic of events" will require that certain agreements shall be made and kept, respecting the land which each tribe shall occupy, and thus arises a system of law. It is true that many tribes will band together for the pillage or conquest of unfriendly neighbors, and, this being accomplished, the nation becomes larger, more complex. Its industries become diversified. Its people have a national feeling. A man is proud to be called a Greek or a Roman. Foreign wars of conquest are attempted. The weakest people must acknowledge the power of Rome. Providence is on the side of the strongest battalions.

That this law holds true throughout the phenomena of mind will be observed when examining the motives which lead men to action. Shall I walk to the lake or to the forest, as the sum of attractions at either place is greater, other things being equal, in that direction I am led. The choice of motives is always along the line of least resistance, though the object to be attained is often remote and the obstacles to be overcome numerous. Witness the long and arduous duties through which a lawyer will willingly pass, in order to win a case or to attain a judgeship.

Likewise, with thought upon any subject, the strongest reasons invariably attract and hold our belief. We think that which is easiest for us to think, whether true or not; but when our error is pointed out, the truth becomes easier to believe and the opinion is rectified.

Even among those who are supposed to be without rational thought, the law holds with equal force. The insane show by their ravings that the forces of the mind run to their strongest or weakest passions, such as fear, love, jealousy, and the like.

The law of the Survival of the Fittest is but another expression of the subject in hand. Those surviving who are the strongest and best fitted for living in their environment, which is equivalent to saying that life moves along the line of greatest traction or least resistance, or of their resultant. Do we not see civilization advancing along those lines where the tractive forces are the greatest, where the least labor will produce the largest crops, and where the obstacles to complete living are the fewest?

Do not people invest their money where it will safely bring the largest returns? Do we not buy in the cheapest, and sell in the dearest market? Does not the tide of immigration set from least favored nations to the most favored?

Between any number of forces acting upon a body there must exist some relation. If they are all equal, and opposite, the body remains stationary, and, to say that the body would move under these conditions is to say that some force has come into existence, which before was not, — which is to say, that something has come out of nothing. This is inconceivable.

If they are not equal and opposite, each force will influence each other force, till the resultant forces are practically reduced to two, and, as between the two resultant forces, motion will take the line of the greatest traction or of the least resistance.

To further multiply examples would be much like adding proof to certainty, and, as there can be no certainty greater than is the truth that force is indestructible, so there is no truth more certain than that, as between forces, motion takes the line of least resistance. This truth does not hold alone of one class of phenomena, but is applicable to all classes, from star clusters to molecules. We see it illustrated about us every day, in innumerable ways. We cannot find a single case where it does not apply. We cannot conceive how motion can take place in any other direction than is specified in the formula.

In fact, the proposition that motion takes the line of least resistance, or greatest traction, or their resultant, may be considered an ultimate fact of knowledge, as true and substantial as is our positive knowledge of existence.

CHAPTER II.

THE RHYTHM OF MOTION.

When, from the deck of a steamer, one looks at the furrow or path of the vessel, as it ploughs its way through the sea, he observes that the wake, as it is called, spreading away from him for a considerable distance, is always a serpentine line. If he is a man of business, he probably blames the steersman for using time and fuel in making such an indirect course, and, being told that the pilot is one of the best on the water and perfectly competent, he begins to ask himself the cause. To the forward motion, imparted by the revolving screw, he adds the deflections caused by the constant influence of the waves and the currents, the force of the wind, and the unequal shape of the sides of the vessel, all which must be balanced from minute to minute by the influence of the rudder and, as the forces at work are never equal, but always vary; he concludes that the path consequently can never be straight.

Another example of rhythm in moving bodies may be observed in the moving railroad train, the start, the swinging motion from side to side, to which add those lateral motions which occur as the cars gain in speed, and the finish. The boy, too, with his ear to the track, has discovered, long before it came in sight, that the train was coming, by the waves of sound which the vibrations of the wheels have sent to him.

The ocean is never quiet. The billows bear waves upon their bosoms, which in turn are ruffled by wavelets and drops of spray. The wavelike appearance of sand dunes, the rolling billows chasing each other up the long beach, and, when the tide goes out, the appearance of the ribbed sea sand, show us further examples of motion along curved lines. Rivers and creeks never flow in straight lines, and even when channels are cut, and the water let into them, there is commenced a wearing away here and an addition there that will eventually change the original straight course to one made up of curves. The eddies and whirlpools, which from moment to moment form and disappear, show how impossible it is for running water not to be thrown into rhythmic motions. The waterfall shows us another example in the curved appearance of the rapids above the falls, the slowly bending circle which it is beginning to make as it takes its final leap, and the rushing and roar of the falling waters is, at a distance, heard as a low musical note.

The winds do not blow steadily, but come in gusts of greater or less force. The leaves quiver in the silent air; the boughs sway to and fro with rhythmic motion in the awakening breeze, and in a violent storm the trembling of the house shows that a certain rhythm has been imparted to it. Storms move usually in circles, and have been compared to wheels that, while revolving themselves, have also a forward motion. This phenomenon has been accurately observed by the United States Signal Service. Reports, stating the directions of the wind, are received from a large number of stations scattered over an immense stretch of territory. Upon a raised map the stations are marked by small arrows, and these arrows are turned in the direction toward which the wind is blowing as the reports come in from the different stations. The appearance of the arrows shows a circle which corresponds to the actual movement of the atmosphere. Vessels at sea, sailing west, with the wind upon the starboard, have passed through the centre of storms, which is marked by a calm, and encountered the wind upon the left or larboard side.

Cyclones show this spiral arrangement in the funnel-shaped mass which they present.

Sound is produced by the vibration of bodies, and is therefore a mode of motion. When we speak, we do not blow the air from our lungs, but condense it before the mouth and throw it into vibrations. When a bell is rung, or a whistle blown, the vibrations do not come to us in straight lines, but in long or short waves, according to the pitch of the tone. When a metal plate, sprinkled with fine sand, is made to vibrate by drawing a violin bow across its edge, the sand will begin to move and dance, and arrange itself in rhythmic geometrical figures. That music and musical sounds consist of rhythmic vibrations hardly needs to be pointed out. Even friction is rhythmical; the flying bullet sings as softly as a bird.

Heat, being also a mode of motion, conforms to the same laws as sound, in that it moves in waves and can be radiated, reflected, absorbed, and focussed. The same can also be said concerning light, which travels in shorter and quicker waves. Whether or not electricity is the highest mode of motion that we know, we at least are sure that in its manifestations it presents a rhythm. We know that the aurora, an electrical phenomenon, dances in time to the varying sun-spots, and that magnetic storms obey the same changing influence.

The magnetic needle does not point steadily in the same direction, but is subject to daily oscillations. During the early part of the day the north pole of the needle moves towards the west, and returns to its mean position about 10 P. M. This daily movement is greater in summer, in our latitude, than in winter, and this diurnal oscillation increases and decreases pretty regularly during a period of about eleven years. The maximum and minimum of this period of magnetic disturbance is found to coincide with the maximum and minimum of the sun-spot period. But, it may be objected, there are certainly some motions which are not rhythmical. Witness, for instance, at Creedmore,. the flight of the rifle-ball from the shooting-station to the target. It is replied that the bullet, when it leaves the gun, is beginning an extremely elliptical circle, having the earth for its central point, and which would be completed but for the resistance offered by the atmosphere and the strong gravitative force which the earth presents. While, on starting out, we thought this might be an exception, it turns out be an excellent illustration. There are the waves of sound produced by the discharge of the powder; the whizz of the shot as it flies toward the mark; the parabolic curve, reaching, at its highest point on the thousand-yard range, about seventy-five feet above the target; and lastly, those thermal undulations caused when the bullet strikes the iron.

Astronomy furnishes examples of rhythm in stars that alternately brighten and fade; in planets that move through immense ellipses; in comets that come and go with great regularity, and the spiral arrangement of the nebulæ show a marked and unmistakable rhythm.

The revolving earth causes the rhythm of light and darkness, periods at which the daily temperature reaches its maximum and minimum, and in its journey about the sun occur the rhythms of the seasons, Spring, Summer, Autumn, and Winter, when the yearly temperature of any place touches the highest and lowest points; regularly recurring periods, when the globe reaches its perihelion, or point nearest the sun, and its aphelion, or point most distant from the sun. To which can be added the rhythm called Nutation, caused by the gyratory motion of the earth not being regular and uniform, which is completed in about nineteen years, and the rhythm called Precession of the Equinoxes, which is completed in about twenty-six thousand years. The moon moving about the earth is an example of compound rhythm, — lesser rhythms included in larger; for, to its own motion about our globe must be added the motion of the earth around the sun, and that far greater rhythm, the motion of the sun itself toward the constellation of Hercules.

That the formation of mountain chains presents a certain rhythm, we must admit when we see them extending along lines more or less irregular, and raising their summits to greater or less altitudes; also the approaches which lead to mountains from opposite sides, and which are sometimes called foot-hills, consist in most cases of waves of rock and soil that face each other. Another character of mountains is formed by the erosive power of rivers, and these also present a certain rhythm as regards height and contour.

The third variety, those formed by volcanic action, appearing as they do in regions where the earth's crust is the weakest, or where the internal pressure is the greatest, and having their periods of eruption at approximately equal intervals, and the well-known wave motion of the ground during an earthquake, — these, and like facts would lead us to infer that, among phenomena classed as geological, as well as among phenomena classed as astronomical, rhythm is a necessary companion of motion. We have not referred to the marked rhythm of the spouting geysers in the Yellowstone region and in Iceland, or to the gradual sinking in some places of the soil, and elevation in other places, or to the successive layers of different silts at the mouths of rivers, causing variations in strata, or of the rhythm both as regards position on and in the earth's crust of mineral deposits; for to mention all the evidences would manifestly swell this volume to large proportions, as well as tire the reader with almost endless repetition.

That vegetation also exhibits rhythmical motion will be observed when we remember that certain plants have had their periods of growth and decay; when we remember the curved rootlets, the circular trunks and branches, and the annular rings which they exhibit. Leaves, in all varieties of shapes, with small branches running from the stem of each leaf, at regular distances, which in turn support still smaller branchlets and delicate veins, present a certain symmetry of arrangement which points to the same conclusion. The color, too, of the leaves in Autumn, consisting of all shades of red, yellow, and brown, slowly melting into each other and appearing in different parts of the forest, and upon certain branches of trees and not upon others, show us, although we may not understand the process, that there is a rhythm of color which answers to the forces and movements that have caused it.

Animal life is rhythmic. From the evidences in the earth's crust we know that after an age of fire has come an age when molluscs and fishes were abundant, after which period came the time when the present coal beds were formed, called the Carboniferous Age; then followed the age when reptiles were numerous, and then one in which mammals flourished, and, lastly the Quarternary or Age of Man; ages distinguished from each other by the fact that the special product of such ages slowly advanced to its maximum, and then as slowly declined to its minimum.

Animals, in ranging over a country where food is plentiful and enemies are few, will increase in numbers, and, as their food, from any cause, becomes less abundant and their enemies numerous, will decrease in numbers. Without entering into a detailed examination of the facts, the evidence is sufficiently strong to say that animal life on the globe has not been one period of uninterrupted advance, but is composed of advances and subsidences extending over long periods of time. It is also to be noticed that what may be said of animal life in general applies, with equal force, to each species which may be considered. That the human race exhibits periods of rise, fall, and decay, it suffices to mention the melancholy names of Jerusalem, Alexandria, Athens, and Rome. Each race distinct. Each history closed forever. Along with the rise and fall of peoples and governments has gone the rise and fall of religions. "'T was Jove's, 't is

Mahomet's, and other creeds will rise with other years." There are periods in which art and philosophy have flourished, followed by the Dark Ages, whence again arise literature and science. Periods in which wars are frequent, to be followed by times of peace. Periods in which the subjective sciences prevail, and periods when the objective sciences demand attention.

So, too, with the standards by which commerce has been carried on, has there been an ebb and flow. Coins of gold, silver, and copper have been in use as money for over twenty-five hundred years, and their buying power has been in the order in which they are named. An ounce of gold has been more valuable than an ounce of silver, and this than an ounce of copper. But their relative value has never been permanent, even where the law has sought to discover and fix it.

In Greece, gold was reckoned as one to twelve and a half of silver. In Rome, copper was the original standard, and afterward silver. In Cæsar's time gold became the standard, and was reckoned as one to twelve of silver, and in the reign of Alexander Severus gold became the sole standard throughout the Roman Empire. After the downfall of that Empire, gold maintained itself for a time in France and Spain, but silver gradually regained its lost place in Europe, to be again gradually displaced by gold as a standard. In 1717 a double standard was established in Great Britain, gold being rated to silver as one to about fifteen, and in 1816 gold was made the sole standard.[1] The present ratio of gold to silver is about one to nineteen.

In society the tendency that is continually shown to revert to former styles has given rise to the somewhat trite observation that fashions are rhythmical, undergoing oscillations from one extreme to the other. Dancing consists in the rhythmic motion of the limbs and body to the sound of music, and that music which allows the easiest and most natural arrangement of the limbs in keeping time is commonly conceded to be the best. The exhilaration, too, which it produces consists of an ebb and flow, and that the conversation of an evening party will alternate between times of activity and times of comparative quiet, has probably been within the notice of all.

In poetry the presence of rhythm is marked, and upon examining prose writings we shall find a sequence of sentence to consist of long, short, and medium, and each sentence will be further divided into parts where the voice rises or falls, where the stop between propositions is sufficiently long to count from one to six; and if the words which compose the separated propositions be examined, they will be found to consist of smaller rhythms of sound, put together to represent the thought for which the word stands. Similarly with the ideas which sentences convey to us, there is a constant ebb and flow. The sentence

---

[1] Perry's "Elements of Political Economy."

begins: each word, as it comes to our view, suggests a conception which is modified by each succeeding word, till the climax of the idea to be conveyed is reached, whence the sentence gradually sinks to its end. Indeed, we hear it frequently remarked that the speaker's or writer's sentences "are well rounded," a tacit recognition that the writing and speaking of sentences is rhythmic.

Does the law of ryhthm stop here? By no means. To the phenomena external to man, which we have been examining for evidence of rhythm, we must now add the phenomena included in his life and acts. We know that men are born, and gradually increase in growth to a maximum of powers, and then gradually decline till death; that included in this greater rhythm are periods of work and of rest, and times of hunger and repletion; times of sickness and of health; and these, when closely examined, are found to consist of still smaller rhythms. Health is not one continuous joyful existence. There are times when work is pleasant, and times when it lags and is disagreeable. Sickness does not consist of one unyielding pain, but of times when it rises into agony and then slowly subsides. In recognition of this fact some diseases have been named intermittent. Convalescents do not get uniformly better, but have their days of partial relapse. The food that is taken at recurrent meals follows a rhythmic course through the intestines, and, by its oxidation and assimilation — processes which upon close examination are found to be admirable examples of rhythm — keeps alive the heartbeats and the rhythmic inspiration and expiration of the breath. Men in good health increase and decrease in weight continually. Athletes, when highly trained, never keep their full power for a long time, but slowly retrograde and again advance.

The phenomena of life, births, marriages, when tabulated and reduced to diagrams, show vast ascents and descents, each extending over a period of years. The applause and uproar of large assemblies of men, such as are engaged, for instance, in making Presidential nominations, rises wave upon wave of sound, and slowly sinks again to quiet.

In short, the proposition that all motion is rhythmical is recognized as one of the profoundest scientific truths of the day.

To suppose a straight course possible, we must conceive of a body moving through a boundless space, void of all influence save that of the moving body. This is inconceivable. And as we must conceive of every body as influenced by more than one force, we must admit that rhythm is a necessary concomitant of motion. The simplest method has been used in the exposition of the proposition, that of example, and it has indeed proved to be the most powerful, as, in selecting illustrations from a great variety of phenomena, we are unable to find a case in which our propositions do not apply. Indeed, that character of mind which could formulate the law of the direction of motion as here set forth in opposite terms might well be worthy of admiration, and, though possible to be formulated in words, it could by no means be rendered into thought.

Our position, then, is, that rest is nowhere ; that, wherever we find motion, that motion is in the line of least resistance, or of greatest traction, or of their resultant, and that motion always is rhythmical.

THE SCIENCE OF BUSINESS.

PART II.

CHAPTER I.

GENERAL BUSINESS.

OF all the phenomena of trade, there are none more obvious or remarkable, or which have attracted greater attention, than fluctuations in price. These are what render business so attractive to the great body of men who engage in it. The fact that the value of a stock of goods may be increased oftentimes twenty or thirty per cent, without any effort upon the part of the holder, offers to many men particular inducements which are resisted with difficulty. Agriculture and the mechanical arts, it is true, hold out the promise of a comfortable existence, if enthusiastically followed, but in times of peace it is principally by trade that wealth is amassed.

Farmers, however, are not simply producers of wheat and other grains, but all trade and traffic, more or less. Lawyers, doctors, schoolmasters, mechanics, and even clergymen, buy and sell houses and lots, and dabble in stocks, and in so far as they do these things, by which property is exchanged, they may be classed as business men.

But while a business man can always be truthfully and adequately described as an exchanger of commodities, the business itself, the process of exchange, will be found, upon close examination, to consist of a series of motions gone through with by men for the purposes of gain.

The dealer in furs, after having, by a certain series of movements, cured, dyed, and softened the skin of the seal, moves his shears through the hide and fashions it into a garment, which, by another series of movements, is exchanged for money. In order to keep his business from a standstill, he must have a continual supply of new hides, and this demand generates upon the part of other men certain other motions, such as sailing to distant seas, bartering with natives for skins; or those laborious and complex motions are generated, by which seals are either captured alive, killed and skinned, or shot from a row-boat while sleeping upon the icebergs of an arctic sea.

The lumberman, who makes it his business to cut timber, bring it to the market, and prepare it for the operations of the carpenter, from the beginning to the end of his operations. goes through motions suitably hinged together to accomplish this ultimate purpose. He moves himself and his men to a place where trees abound. He directs — by the motion of his hands in pointing, and his lips in speaking — which trees shall be felled. His assistants, by well-directed movements of their arms in swinging axes, cut through the trunks of the trees, and the attraction of gravity brings the timber to the ground, The sawyers move a saw through the trees and divide them into logs of convenient size. Horses and men, by the expenditure of a certain force, move the logs to the river, from whose waters they are again taken, and when the mill-saw has moved its way through the log, the timber is in such shape as will best serve the wants of the carpenter and builder, who, by going through certain other motions, fashion sidewalks, fences, or dwellings.

Again, if we inquire concerning the process by which the engine which utilizes the steam-power and drives the saw through the logs has come to its present shape, we shall find that the iron of which it is composed once existed as a dull-red, earthy deposit, and that it has been moved by shovels and barrows, placed in the hold of a vessel, and moved to the blast-furnace, whence it issues as pig iron. And this product, being subject to certain movements directed by men, such as being cast, hammered, filed, turned upon a lathe, etc., the perfected shape at last results, and the manufacture of stationary engines, thus carried on by going through motions which shape iron into engines, constitutes an important branch of the iron trade. How true this is, that all business consists of motions, each one may readily determine for himself. Let him who doubts this statement go to his office in the morning and refrain from any motions whatever; let him refuse to sign checks, write orders, sell bills to customers, and give directions to clerks,—all which require an expenditure of force, and therefore a generation of motion,—and see how much business he will accomplish. Seriously, then, without undertaking an extended exposition, we may safely assert that no business, no process of exchange, can be carried on without motions, and that the purpose for which such motions are gone through with is some kind of a gain, —usually of money, of credit, or of property. Let the purpose be what it may, the motions which each business man goes through are in the line of least resistance, or of the greatest traction, or of their resultant, and they are also rhythmical.

Mr. H—— lives in a town where a large number of cars, rails, and locomotives are made. The people who labor in the shops require meats and vegetables for their daily food, whence arises a demand—a tractive force—for these articles, which Mr. H—— endeavors to supply. He starts a store and carries a stock of the necessities upon which the laborers live. He furnishes them flour, butter, coffee, sugar, and other articles which necessity or fancy dictates, and in return receives compensation in some representative of value, either labor, property, or money. Whether his sales are large or small depends in some cases upon the rate or price and quality of his goods as compared with the price and quality of his competitor's goods, the customer, other things being equal, patronizing the dealer whose goods, as regards the resultant of price and of quality, are the cheapest.

Not only are the business motions between the retail dealer and his customers in the line of least resistance, but this is also true of the business motions between the retail dealer and wholesale dealer, or jobber as he is sometimes called. The retail dealer always buys his supplies from the party who can furnish him with the best qualities and largest amount of goods at the lowest rates. In addition to quality and price of an article, there may be many factors which determine the business motions between a buyer and a seller, among which may be mentioned the price of freight, the time required to obtain the goods, the risk of loss in the carriage; to which may be added those personal forces which affect some men, such as race, color, nationality, religion, political belief, education, and the age and reputation of the seller. Some business men will have no dealings with Jews, some are averse to buying goods of negroes, and, in times of great political excitement, some will rather buy of those of the same political belief. These, although they may not be all, are a few of the causes which determine business motions, to which must be added those latent forces, difficult to point out, but which are evident from their effect. Upon examination and comparison of all these forces which regulate the exchange of commodities, we at last arrive at the formula which our law specifies — motion in the line of the least resistance, or of the greatest traction, or of their resultant.

Moreover, the business motions which we are here

considering are rhythmic. Making use again of the foregoing illustration, we see that the number of laborers in the town must be continually increasing or diminishing through emigration or immigration, birth, sickness, or death, requiring constantly an ever-changing amount of food, which generates in the sales of the retailer like rhythms, extending, it may be, over days, weeks, months, and years. The sales are probably the largest and most profitable when the demand is the largest, and least profitable when the demand is the least. Not only is the exchange of food products influenced by the number and wants of laborers, but also by the number and wants of all other exchangers, dealers in boots and shoes, clothing, coal, crockery, dry goods, drugs, jewelry, etc., each business showing days of large and small sales, months and years when business is dull or brisk, corresponding to the increased or lessened demand. Nor is it to the laboring classes that all business men look for trade. The boot and shoe man sells not only to the laborer, but also to all other business men. The dry-goods man traffics with the jeweler, the jeweler with the druggist, and all with the grocer. Each trades with the other, and endeavors to fill his desires with the least effort, directed to the greatest gain.

A fact to be noted here is that the interests of all men are intertwined. Formerly, all a farmer prayed for was abundant crops. If he had large flocks of sheep and herds of cattle, he was happy. If his granaries were well filled and his swine were fat, he was rich. Now the aspect is different. Then he made his own clothes and supplied his wants with the labor of his own hands. Now he finds that, owing to the specialization of labor, he can buy his boots, clothes, and agricultural implements with less trouble and of a better quality than he can himself make them. He now wants a market. He must not only produce, but he must sell. He is no longer the independent being represented by the poets. He sends his wool a thousand miles, it may be, to be spun into cloth. The hides of his cattle are rarely directly utilized by him. His grain is shipped to distant cities, where it is made into bread which keeps alive the employees of the manufacturer, who supplies him with ploughs, rakes, reapers, windmills, and the thousand and one articles which he has now found to be an absolute necessity in carrying on the work of the farm. In order to successfully compete with other farmers he must abandon the primitive methods of his fathers, he must have iron ploughs, rakes, and reapers, and for these things he is dependent upon the manufacturer of these implements, while the manufacturer and his employees are again dependent upon the farmer for the bread they eat and the wages and profits which they respectively receive. Merchants, bankers, stockbrokers, insurance men, and other classes of business men are dependent upon each other and upon the community at large for their profits and for their livelihood, and each finds his own business most satisfactory when all other interests are working smoothly and without commercial discord.

During the growth of an intelligent community new branches of business are constantly arising. Within the last hundred years have come the railroad, the electric telegraph, and the telephone. Pig iron has been turned to steel, corn is made into syrup, and dyes, rivalling the colors of the rainbow, are made from coal-tar. With the increased number and complexity of business occupations has come the specialization of labor. One man devotes his life to building railroads, another to making the rails, another to furnishing the cars and locomotives. In the use of electricity some are engaged in telegraphy, others in electric lighting, others in electric railroading. A large class of men are engaged in lumbering, in mining for metals, coal, petroleum, and salt, in making glassware, in manufacturing pottery, iron implements for household use, and stoves. There are men who make brick, and men who lay them, roofers and slaters, plasterers, plumbers, gas-fitters, blacksmiths, brass-founders, cabinet-makers, cigar-makers, hatters, clothiers, saddle-makers and harness-makers, goldsmiths and tinsmiths, coopers, draymen, stevedores, and other trades. Each business of any considerable extent is again subdivided into specialties. Thus the locomotive builder must employ travelling agents, book-keepers, time-keepers, watchmen, draughtsmen, machinists, moulders, blacksmiths, boiler-makers, brass-workers, carpenters, iron finishers, pattern makers, riveters, joiners, painters, and laborers. Any large industry, when carefully examined, will be found to exhibit the truth that the tendency of advancing civilization is toward a specialization of industry.

This division of labor has given a vast increase to that class of men who constitute the medium of exchange — the mercantile classes. Primitive merchants were simply hawkers of wares, dealers in a few simple commodities, travelling through the land bartering and trading for whatever had value to them. Now the mercantile classes are a body, dependent, it is true, upon the producer of food, great in numbers, and as diversified in character as are the wants or fancies of the populace which they endeavor to supply.

Everybody is aware how much the interests of the mercantile classes and other classes are affected by fluctuations in value. Fortunes are made or lost by the rise or fall in price of a commodity of which a merchant may have a large supply. But the merchant is affected not only by the price of articles in his possession, but by the price of articles in the possession of others. He owes a large number of people and a large number of people owe him. His ability to pay depends upon the prices which his customers receive for the produce or goods they have in their possession, or which their debtors produce or have in their possession. Hence there is hardly a fluctuation in the price of any article whatsoever that does not influence to some extent the prosperity of the mercantile classes at large, in addition to the particular influence which it may exert upon the fortunes of a particular individual. In society as we see it to-day, not only each man is dependent upon other men, but each class of men is dependent upon all other classes, and whatever injures one class of the community effects upon all other classes a like injury. The interests of each are bound up in the interests of all, and the interest of all is bound up in the interest of each.

Considering the business of a community as a whole, made up of innumerable motions, diversified, intricate, we are forced to conclude that the general movement of business in that community must be along the line of least resistance. As has been before pointed out, any number of motions, when brought together, must at last be reduced to two, — that of attraction and that of counter-attraction, and, in the direction of greatest force, motion takes place. Not only, then, must the business which each individual performs be increasing or decreasing, but also the total business done by all individuals; and, as motion cannot take place in one direction forever, we must expect a constant reversal of motion between limits, or a rhythm.

Turning from philosophy to fact, we find that it is the common experience of business men that times are "good," and times are "bad," meaning that exchange of commodities is active or slow. Some attribute the cause to the crops, others to overproduction, others to the influence of the tariff, and others to the political party which may happen to be in power. Without at present examining the adequacy of the several commonly supposed causes to produce the observed effects, we have no hesitancy in saying that times cannot be uniformly good, neither can they be uniformly bad.

The number of failures in business is probably as good if not the best exponent of the commercial prosperity of the country, as any index that we have. At least, it will be admitted that that state of affairs which should cause one man among every one hundred and sixty-six traders to fail in one year is much preferable to that state of affairs which should cause one man, in the same time, to fail among every sixty-seven traders. Embracing, as they do, every class of business men, and extending over a large territory, we may expect that such a record of failures will express a general truth ; and, from the course of reasoning heretofore followed, we may expect that the number of failures for any year will not be a fixed quantity. That, viewed singly or collectively, they will show the movement of forces along the lines of least resistance or of greatest traction, and we may also expect that they will present a certain rhythm. That they do present a rhythm, the annexed diagram of the average of failures for each year from 1866–1885 will graphically show. The data from which the diagram is plotted are as follows : —

THE SCIENCE OF BUSINESS.

Year.	Traders.	Failures.	Amount of Liabilities.	Average of Liabilities.	Average of Failures.
1857		4,932	$291,750,000		
1858		4,225	95,749,000		
1859		3,913	64,394,000		
1860		3,676	79,807,000		
1861		6,993	207,210,000		
1862		1,652	23,049,000		
1863		495	7,899,000		
1864		520	8,579,000		
1865		530	17,625,000		
1866	160,303	1,505	53,783,000	$35,736	1 in 106
1867	205,000	2,780	96,666,000	34,772	1 in 74
1868	276,000	2,608	68,694,000	26,339	1 in 105
1869	355,000	2,799	75,054,000	26,813	1 in 126
1870	427,292	3,546	88,242,000	24,885	1 in 120
1871	476,018	2,915	85,252,000	21,775	1 in 163
1872	532,236	4,069	121,056,000	29,750	1 in 130
1873	562,054	5,183	228,499,000	44,084	1 in 108
1874	603,904	5,830	155,239,000	26,627	1 in 103
1875	644,389	7,740	201,000,000	25,969	1 in 83
1876	680,072	9,092	191,117,000	21,020	1 in 75
1877	689,000	8,872	190,670,000	21,491	1 in 77
1878	713,420	10,478	234,383,000	22,369	1 in 67
1879	751,235	6,658	98,149,000	14,741	1 in 111
1880	787,480	4,735	65,752,000	13,886	1 in 166
1881	810,485	5,582	81,156,000	14,530	1 in 145
1882	847,795	6,738	101,548,000	15,070	1 in 126
1883	869,170	9,184	172,874,000	18,823	1 in 94
1884	937,974	10,968	226,343,000	20,637	1 in 86

We are indebted to R. G. Dun & Co. for above statement of failures and liabilities.

GENERAL BUSINESS.

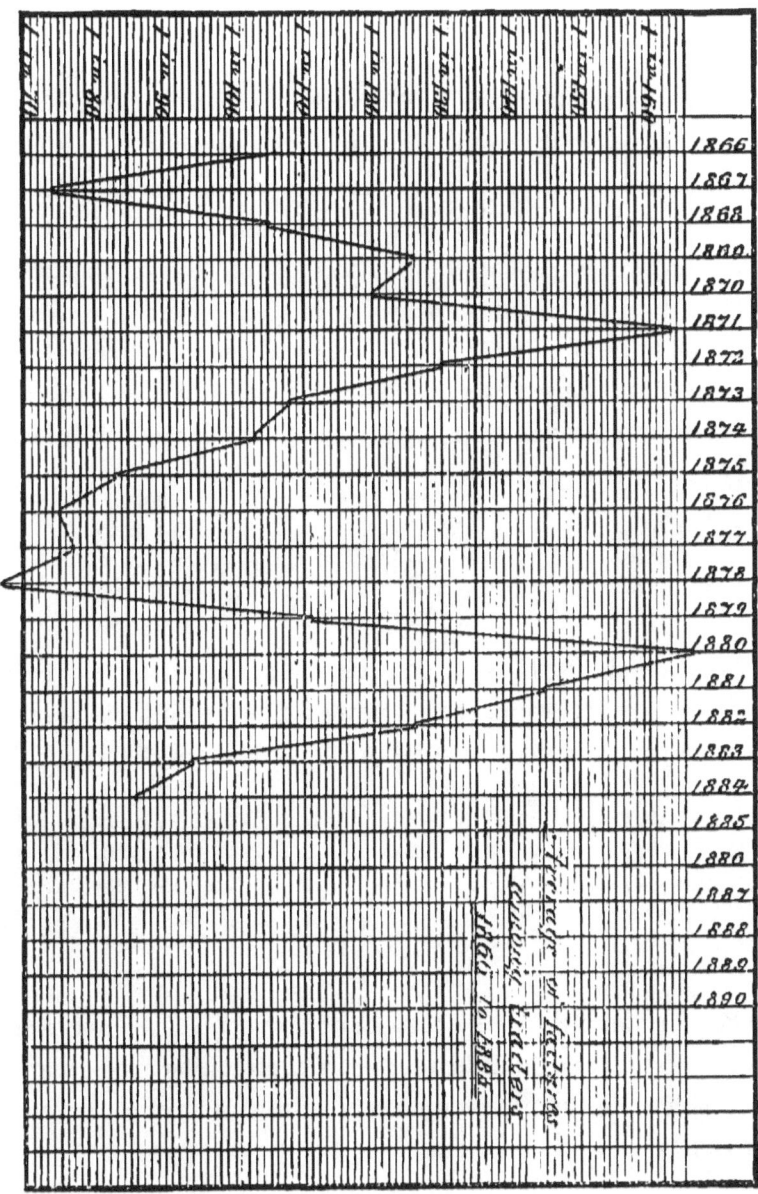

It will be noticed, upon examining the chart, that the upward movement from a low average to a high average of failures is quick, sharp, and decisive, and that the downward movements from the highest points reached are slow and easy descents, extending over a period of years. Along with the rise and fall in the average number of traders who fail yearly has gone a like rise and fall in yearly liabilities. Thus, if we take the period of four years when the average of failures was above 1 in 110, the mean between the highest and lowest average, we find that they divide themselves into periods of relatively small and large liabilities. Thus the four years —

	Liabilities.
1869	$75,054,000
1870	88,242,000
1871	85,252,000
1872	121,056,000

show a liability of $369,604,000, or an average per year of $92,401,000, while the six years following, and which fall below the average of one failure to 110 traders —

	Liabilities.
1873	$228,499,000
1874	155,239,000
1875	201,000,000
1876	191,117,000
1877	190,670,000
1878	234,383,000

show a liability of $1,200,908,000, or a yearly average of $200,151,333; and the four years again following — years in which the average number of failures is again above 1 to 110 —

	Liabilities.
1879	$98,149,000
1880	65,752,000
1881	81,156,000
1882	101,548,000

show liabilities amounting to $346,605,000 or a yearly average of $86,651,250. When follow the years of —

	Liabilities.
1883	$172,874,000
1884	226,343,000

with yearly average liabilities of $199,608,500, which brings us down to the present time.

That this state of affairs is about to change now, and again advance, we have no reason to believe. As was pointed out in the chapter on the rhythm of motion, we are led to suspect that we have entered a period of business depression which is to last for several years before any decided change for the better can take place.[1] That action and reaction are opposite and equal we cannot doubt. The even and exact method of natural law must take its course. The rhythm must be completed.

Within the greater rhythms are included lesser, which rise and sink upon the larger billows; thus the percentage number of failures to the year has been found to be always greater in the first quarter of the year than in the last three quarters, as the following table will show : —

---

[1] The duration of this period of depression will be treated in a subsequent chapter.

Year.	First Quarter. Percentage of failures to year.	Second Quarter. Percentage of failures to year.	Third Quarter. Percentage of failures to year.	Fourth Quarter. Percentage of failures to year.
1876	30.86	19.73	26.95	22.46
1877	32.34	21.19	20.47	26.00
1878	32.02	23.57	27.23	17.18
1879	37.91	23.04	18.95	20.10
1880	30.24	22.49	20.68	26.59
1881	31.55	19.80	18.34	30.31
1882	31.57	21.82	19.29	27.32
1883	30.72	19.77	19.63	29.88
1884	30.05	20.19	21.39	28.37

(The above table was first prepared by the publishers of the New York *Financial Review*.)

With the exception of 1879, the percentage of failures for the first quarter has been about thirty-one per cent of the year's total. Knowing this fact enables us to predict with reasonable accuracy the total number of failures for the year from the number of failures in the first quarter. This rule, however, is of questionable value, as the data upon which it is based have not as yet been extended over a sufficient number of years. The fact, however, which we have endeavored to impress is that the number of failures for any quarter is not an equal percentage of the year's failures, but shows a yearly rhythm.

Another point to be noticed is that, as a rule, the failures of the fall and winter months bear a larger proportion to the year's failures than do the failures of the spring and summer months. The percentages are as follows:—

Year.	Fall and Winter Months.	Spring and Summer Months.
1876	53.32	46.68
1877	58.34	41.66
1878	49.20	50.80
1879	58.01	41.99
1880	56.83	43.17
1881	61.86	38.14
1882	58.89	41.11
1883	60.60	39.40
1884	58.42	41.58

The percentage of failures of first and last quarter is about 57 per cent of year's total.

Previous to the year 1866 we have no reliable information, either as to the number of traders in business or the number of failures; still the record furnished by commercial history is sufficient to show us that commercial panics and periods of distress have been rhythmic; and while they may not furnish us with a knowledge of the exact truth, still the information has some value; a value, however, not to be compared with that positive and exact statement which figures enable us to furnish. In England, during the years 1811 and 1812, trade was brisk, and from 1814 to 1816 commercial distress prevailed. Toward the close of 1824 it was observed that the rate of consumption of some of the leading articles was outrunning the supply, and thus an incentive was afforded the spirit of speculation. Every one bought. Speculation in foreign shares and loans took place to an extent never before known. Joint-stock companies were formed for every conceivable purpose. Three companies were formed for working the Mexican mines, and similar companies for working the mines of Chili, Brazil, Peru, and the provinces of the Rio de la Plata, and for prosecuting the pearl fisheries on the coast of Columbia. In the language of a writer of that period, "The credulous and the suspicious, the crafty and the bold, the intelligent and the ignorant — princes, nobles, politicians, place-men, patriots, lawyers, physicians, divines, philosophers, poets, intermingled with women of all ranks and degrees, spinsters, wives, and widows, hastened to venture some of their property in schemes of which scarcely anything was known but the name."[1] Commercial discredit and pressure followed in the year 1825, to an extent never known after that time. Five London and seventy country banks stopped payment. The next periods of commercial panics occurred in England in 1837–8, 1847–8, and great depression occurred in both England and the United States in 1857, 1866–67, and 1877 and 1878. And at the present time (October, 1884) the House of Commons has appointed a committee to investigate the causes of the present commercial depression into which we now have entered. The following diagram will show the periods when commercial depression has prevailed : —

---

[1] Hunt's Merchants' Magazine, 1848.

GENERAL BUSINESS. 41

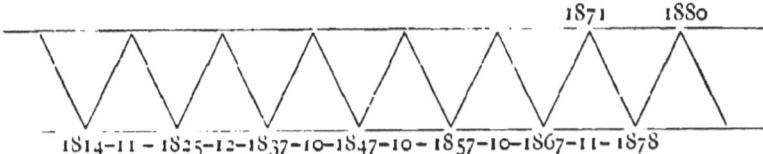

As far as we are able to judge from commercial history, if appears that years of extreme depression are separated from each other by a period of from ten to eleven years. Keeping in view the salient points touched in this chapter, let us turn our attention to the examination of one of the greatest industries of the times, the careful study of which, we may be sure, will amply repay us for the investigation.

CHAPTER II.

IRON.

From the days of Tubal Cain, the production and fashioning of iron has been the distinctive mark of a civilized people, and in the proportion in which the production and uses have increased, in that proportion have the people become more civilized.

"The people of the United States," says Mr. James M. Swank (Census Report, 1880), "are the largest *per capita* consumers of iron and steel in the world, and of all nations are also the largest aggregate consumers of these products. Great Britain makes more iron than we do, but she exports about one half of all that she makes. She exports more than one half of the steel that she makes, and yet makes but little more than this country. No other European country equals Great Britain either in the *per capita* or aggregate consumption of iron and steel.

"A simple enumeration of some of the most important uses to which iron and steel are applied by our people will show how prominent a part these metals play in the development of American civilization, and the advancement of our greatness and power as a nation.

"We have built almost as many miles of railroad as the

whole of Europe, and consequently have used in their construction almost as many rails, and now use almost as many locomotives and cars. At the close of 1881 the United States had nineteen miles of railroad to every ten thousand of population, while Europe had a little more than three miles to the same population. Railroads annually consume more than one half of the world's production of iron and steel, — rails, bridges, cars, and locomotives being impossible without these metals. The street railway is an American invention, which also consumes large quantities of iron and steel, and we were also the first nation to introduce elevated railways to facilitate city travel. We are the foremost of all nations in the use of iron and steel for railroads and ordinary highways, and the lightness and gracefulness of our bridges are nowhere equalled. In the use of iron for water and gas pipes we are probably in advance of any other nation. We make more iron stoves for heating halls and dwellings, and for the purposes of the kitchen, than all the rest of the world. We make liberal use both of cast and of wrought iron in the construction of public and private dwellings. We lead the world in the use of iron and of steel wire for fences, and we have more miles of telegraph wire than any other nation. We use immense quantities of plate iron in the storage, transportation, and refining of petroleum. The oil wells themselves yearly require thousands of tons of iron pipes for tubing. We make liberal use of plate and sheet iron in the construction of chimneys for steamboats on our lakes and rivers, and in the construction of factory, rolling-mill, and blast-furnace chimneys, and the stacks of blast furnaces. Portable and stationary engines and steam fire engines consume large quantities of iron. Anchors and chains, cotton presses and cotton ties, sugar pans and salt pans, and general foundry and machine work, require large quantities of iron and steel. We make our own cotton and woollen manufacturing machinery, and nearly all the other machinery that we use. The manufacture of printing-presses consumes a large quantity of iron.

"We are the leading agricultural nation in the world, and hence are the largest consumers of agricultural implements. Our use of iron and steel in agriculture takes rank next to their use in the construction and maintenance of railroads. We lead all nations in the manufacture of cut-nails, spikes, and tacks. Our extended and varied mining operations consume large quantities of iron and steel, so also do our manufactures of scales and balances, letter-presses, burglar and fire proof safes, sewing-machines, wagons and carriages, gratings and street-crossings, lamp-posts, posts for awnings, all sorts of small hardware, horse-shoes and horse-shoe nails, wire rope, iron hoops, iron cots and bedsteads, woven wire mattresses, iron screens, iron railings and stairs, firearms and cannon. In the manufacture of machine and hand tools, and general cutlery, saws, and axes, we enjoy a world-wide reputation. Not the least important use to which iron and steel are put in this country is in the extension of the iron industry itself, — every blast-furnace, rolling-mill, or steel works that is erected, first devouring large quantities of these products before contributing to the general supply."

Along with the increasing number and diversified character of the industries to which iron and steel have been applied, the power of production of these products has increased.

According to the writer whom we have just quoted, fifty years ago the American blast furnace, which would make 4 tons of pig iron in a day, or 28 tons per week, was doing good work. In 1831 it was publicly proclaimed, with some exultation, that "one furnace, erected in Pennsylvania in 1830, will, in 1831, make 1,100 tons of pig iron." But, as George Asmus has well said, "a time came when men were no longer satisfied with these little smelting-pots, into which a gentle stream of air was blown through one nozzle, which received its scant supply from a leather bag squeezed by some tired water-wheel." After 1840 our blast-furnace practice gradually improved; but it was not till 1865 that any furnace in the country could produce 150 tons of pig iron in a week. Ten years later, in 1875, we had several furnaces that could each make 700 tons of pig iron in a week; in 1880 we had several which could each make 1000 tons in a week; and in 1881 we had one furnace which made 224 tons in one day, 1,357 tons in a week, and 5,598 tons in a month.

It is evident, from this hasty and somewhat cursory history of the iron trade, that the production and price of iron constitute important, if not the most important, data concerning the progress of American trade.

Subtract from the history of the country the history of the iron trade, and civilization as we know it to-day would not be possible.

Entering into the life of the nation and of the people; forming, as it does, the sole support of many persons, and the requirement of all, we should expect that a price history and a production history of the iron trade would show us truths of great moment, — truths of as much importance as any that, in a business way, can possibly concern us.

One great factor in the price of pig iron is labor, and it is almost the only factor. As the methods of working the ore grew more scientific, and the yearly output became larger; when steam was introduced to perform the labor formerly done by hand or by horses, in drawing the ore, the coal, and limestone, and when it was discovered that, by heating the blast, iron could be produced quicker and with less coal, the price became gradually less, and to-day we have the anomaly presented to us of better paid labor than fifty years ago, while the yearly *per capita* output has increased probably one thousand per cent.

An examination of the accompanying table and plotted diagram of the price and production of pig iron for a series of years will clearly show that the iron trade has not been a movement of steady growth and increase, but that it consists of rhythms of high and low prices, large and

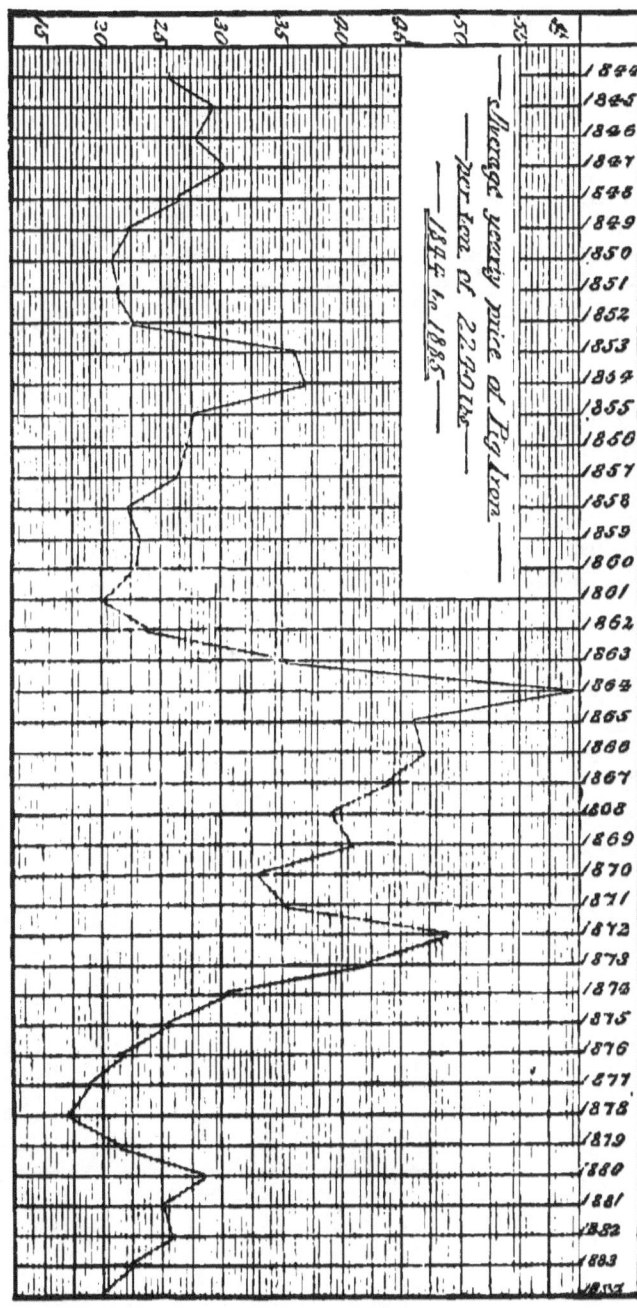

small production, extending over a period of years, which rhythms, like those noted in the previous chapter, are regular in the order in which they recur.

Year.	Average Yearly Price per Ton.	Production of Pig Iron. in U. S. Tons.	Imports of Pig Iron. Tons.	Approximate Consumption of Pig Iron. Tons.	Average Yearly Price of Gold.	Year.
1844	25 3-4					1844
1845	29 1-4				100	1845
1846	27 7-8				100	1846
1847	30 1-4				100	1847
1848	26 1-2				100	1848
1849	22 3-4				100	1849
1850	20 7-8				100	1850
1851	21 3-8				100	1851
1852	22 5-8				100	1852
1853	36 1-8				100	1853
1854	36 7-8				100	1854
1855	27 3-4				100	1855
1856	27 1-8				100	1856
1857	26 3-8				100	1857
1858	22 1-4				100	1858
1859	23 3-8				100	1859
1860	22 3-4	919,770			100	1860
1861	20 1-4	731,544			100	1861
1862	23 7-8	787,662			113	1862
1863	35 1-4	947,604			145	1863
1864	59 1-4	1,135,996			202	1864
1865	46 1-3	931,582			157	1865
1866	46 7-8	1,350,343			140	1866
1867	44 1-8	1,461,626			138	1867
1868	39 1-4	1,603,000			140	1868
1869	40 5-8	1,916,641			135	1869

Year.	Average Yearly Price per Ton.	Production of Pig Iron in U. S. Tons.	Imports of Pig Iron. Tons.	Approximate Consumption of Pig Iron. Tons.	Average Yearly Price of Gold.	Year.
1870	33 1-4	1,865,000			115	1870
1871	35 1-8	1,911,608	245,535	2,157,143	112	1871
1872	48 7-8	2,854,558	295,967	3,150,525	112	1872
1873	42 3-4	2,868,278	154,708	3,022,986	113	1873
1874	30 1-4	2,689,413	61,165	2,750,578	112	1874
1875	25 1-2	2,266,581	83,932	2,350,513	114	1875
1876	22 1-4	2,093,236	83,072	2,176,308	110	1876
1877	18 7-8	2,314,585	66,861	2,381,446	105	1877
1878	17 5-8	2,577,361	74,484	2,651,842	102	1878
1879	21 1-2	3,070,875	340,672	3,411,547	100	1879
1880	28 1-2	4,295,414	784,968	5,080,382	100	1880
1881	25 1-8	4,641,564	520,835	5,162,399	100	1881
1882	25 3-4	5,178,122	604,978	5,783,100	100	1882
1883	22 3-8	5,146,972	361,366	5,508,338	100	1883
1884	20 (Est.)				100	1884

The above table of price, production, etc., of iron was kindly furnished by James M. Swank, Secretary of the American Iron and Steel Association in Philadelphia.

Upon an examination of the chart, we observe that the upward movements have been, like the upward movements in the average of failures, quick and sharp, while the downward movements are long and slow. Thus, in 1844, began an upward movement which culminated in the high-priced year 1847; the downward movement then commenced, which did not receive a decidedly upward tendency till the year 1852. This upward movement came to an end in 1854, and the reaction lasted till 1861. From this point the market rose rapidly to 1864, and again declined to 1870. Again rising to 1872, declined to 1878, from which year began an advance which reached its highest point in 1880, and from that year has steadily declined to the present time.

It will also be noticed that the high-priced years in the iron market are the same as when the average of failures are among the highest years. Thus, when the average yearly price of iron was $48.87½ per ton, in 1872, the average of failures was one (1) to 130 traders, and in 1878, when the yearly average price of iron was $17.62½ per ton, the proportion of failures had increased to 1 among every 67 traders, and in 1880 iron was worth $28.50 per ton, while the number of failures for that year stood in the proportion of 1 to 166 traders.

An examination of the following diagram will show the course of the iron market from its highest to its lowest points, and show the number of years in which it completes a rhythm. It will be noticed that advances from the lowest point have not been less two years or more than three. Declines from highest points have not been less than five nor more than seven years.

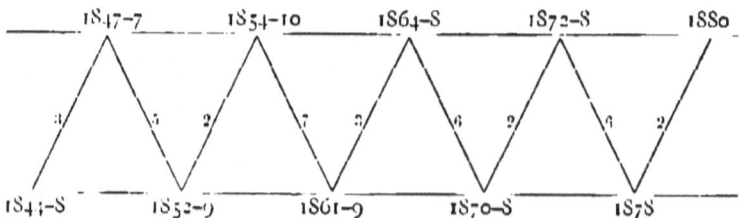

The years of highest prices are separated from each other by intervals of seven, ten, eight, and eight years. The years of lowest prices are separated from each other by intervals of eight, nine, nine, and eight years.

That this remarkable regularity is the result of the tariff, the crops, the policy of political parties, we can hardly believe. That the observed phenomena can be explained as the result of fortuitous circumstances must be left to other pens than mine. In times of war and times of peace, in times of famine and of plenty, still the rhythm moves unbrokenly on. Extending over a long period of years, sufficient to furnish us with reasonable data for a proper judgment, we are led to believe that the movements which we have pointed out must express the true and natural method of the rise and fall of values. This truth is in harmony, not only with that which the record of failures points out, but also with those other truths observable in natural phenomena; truths, into the methods of whose operation we endeavored to give an insight in the chapters contained in Part First — The Direction of Motion and the Rhythm of Motion.

An examination of the production and imports of iron will show us a like truth.

Going back in the history of the trade, as far as the reports of production and of imports are reliable, we find that in the years —

```
1869 . . . . . . . . . . . . . . . . . Not given.
1870 . . . . . . . . . . . . . . . . . Not given.
1871 . . . . . . . . . . . . . . . . . 2,157,143
1872 . . . . . . . . . . . . . . . . . 3,150,525
                                      ─────────
                                   2)5,307,668
                                      ─────────
                                      2,653,834
```

The aggregate consumption of pig iron averaged 2,653,834 tons per year, while the six following years —

```
1873 . . . . . . . . . . . . . . . . . 3,022,986
1874 . . . . . . . . . . . . . . . . . 2,750,578
1875 . . . . . . . . . . . . . . . . . 2,350,513
1876 . . . . . . . . . . . . . . . . . 2,176,308
1877 . . . . . . . . . . . . . . . . . 2,381,446
1878 . . . . . . . . . . . . . . . . . 2,651,842
                                      ──────────
                                   6)15,333,673
                                      ──────────
                                      2,555,612
```

show an annual average of 2,555,612 tons; and if we take into account the enormous gain in population during those six years, we should expect that the annual consumption should have been much greater, and the fact that it averaged less can only be explained by saying that, as compared with the previous four years, business in those six years was poor.

The four years following —

```
1879 . . . . . . . . . . . . . . . . . 3,411,547
1880 . . . . . . . . . . . . . . . . . 5,080,382
1881 . . . . . . . . . . . . . . . . . 5,162,399
1882 . . . . . . . . . . . . . . . . . 5,783,100
                                      ──────────
                                   4)19,437,428
                                      ──────────
                                      4,859,357
```

show an annual average of 4,859,357 tons, while the years 1883 and 1884 show a decided falling off in consumption from the highest point reached in 1882.

CHAPTER III.

RAILROAD BUILDING.—CONSUMPTION OF IRON AND STEEL RAILS.

AT the commencement of the year 1884 there were, in the United States, 121,494 miles of railroad in operation, which, at the moderate estimate of $40,000 per mile, would represent an investment of nearly $5,000,000,000.[1] Of this amount 33,705 miles were built previous to 1864, representing, at $40,000 per mile, $1,348,200,000; and 87,789 miles were built since the close of the year 1863, representing, at $40,000 per mile, $3,511,560,000.

During this latter period, which commences with the year 1864 and extends to the year 1884, 74 per cent of the railroad mileage of the country was built. This period, upon examination, divides itself into four distinct divisions of five years each, two of rapid and two of moderate, railroad building, as follows:—

TWO PERIODS OF MODERATE RAILROAD BUILDING.

	Miles		Miles
1864	738	1874	1,105
1865	1,177	1875	1,712
1866	1,742	1876	2,712
1867	2,449	1877	2,281
1868	2,979	1878	2,687
	9,085		10,497

---

[1] This estimate includes road-beds, rails, rolling-stock, depots, etc. *Poor's Manual* for 1884 shows the amount per mile, as based on bonds and stocks, to be nearer $65,000.

TWO PERIODS OF ACTIVE RAILROAD BUILDING.

	Miles		Miles
1869	4,615	1879	4,721
1870	6,070	1880	7,174
1871	7,379	1881	11,142
1872	5,878	1882	10,821
1873	4,107	1883	6,400
	28,049		40,258

That period from 1864 to 1868 inclusive, in which 9,085 miles were built at a cost of $363,400,000; that period from 1869 to 1873 inclusive, in which 28,049 miles were built, at a cost of $1,121,960,000; that period immediately following, from 1874 to 1878, in which 10,497 miles were built, at a cost of $419,880,000, and that period from 1879 to 1883 inclusive, known in popular language as the "boom," in which 40,258 miles were built, at a cost of $1,610,320,000.

But this estimate of $40,000 per mile as the cost of a railroad is probably too low for the two periods of activity; for iron, steel rails, and wages were much higher during the years from 1879 to 1883 than during the years from 1873 to 1879. Thus, the price of pig iron in November, 1878, was $16.50 per ton, which had risen to $41 in February, 1880. Iron rails rose from $34 in January, 1879, to $68 in February, 1880; and steel rails from $41 in 1878 to $85 in February, 1880, in each case doubling, or more than doubling, the price in a few months. Such was the "boom" of 1879, which caused the building of furnaces, mills, and foundries to supply the increased demand for iron. Prices culminated in February, 1880, but the high prices of steel rails, locomotives, etc., seemed to stimulate instead of to check railroad building.

The amount of money paid out in railroad building from 1879 to 1883, inclusive, at the lowest estimate, must have been considerably over $1,000,000 for each day during the five years, a striking contrast to the $250,000 per day of the previous five years. European and American capitalists paid out over $300,000,000 each year for building railroads in the United States. Of this amount probably one half was paid for labor and for iron, and the balance went to other capitalists, to land, mine, and mill owners, which was again redistributed, and "the end of its influence no man can tell."

As a result of this prosperity wages were high, mills and factories were run on full time, and in many cases all day and night. Iron-working machines could not be built with sufficient rapidity, so they were imported from Europe. Plants of factories were enlarged, new additions were made to the buildings, and the workers were increased. True to the American spirit, each manufacturer strove to get to the market first. The pace was too fast. The producers of railroad material broke the market. They furnished more goods than the capitalists wanted or the people needed, and the natural result followed. Prices fell. In 1884 pig iron had reached $20 per ton, steel rails $28 to $30 per ton, and it is estimated that only about 4,000 miles of railroad were built. This meant the scaling down of wages of all classes of labor connected with railways, the closing of blast furnaces, the shutting up of mills and foundries; for, as we have the capacity to build at least 12,000 miles of railroad in one year, and have only built 4 000, the result is plainly inevitable. We built too many miles in 1879 to 1883, and must build too few in 1884 to 1888 in order to establish an equilibrium.

Nor have we any reason to hope that this regular irregularity will cease, for as soon as an equilibrium is reached and an increased demand springs up, when wages and production have reached their lowest point and turn upward, when profits again become visible to the manufacturer, each blast furnace will be fired up, each mill and foundry will start, and a few years of activity will be again followed by years of depression. Every one who is interested in railway building will endeavor to make hay while the sun shines, and instead of the prosaic and plodding every-day work, on small wages and short hours, incident to depressed business, we shall see activity in every department — the pillar of cloud by day and the pillar of fire by night.

The following table, compiled by the *Railway Gazette*, shows the miles of railroad in operation each year, and the annual increase, from 1830 to 1884. The table of approximate consumption of rails is from the reports of the American Iron and Steel Association at Philadelphia: —

MILES OF RAILROAD IN UNITED STATES.

Year.	Miles in Operation.	Annual Increase.
1830	23	
1831	95	72
1832	229	134
1833	380	151
1834	633	253
1835	1,098	465
1836	1,273	175
1837	1,497	224
1838	1,913	416
1839	2,302	389
1840	2,818	516
1841	3,535	717
1842	4,026	491
1843	4,185	159
1844	4,377	192
1845	4,633	256
1846	4,930	297
1847	5,598	668
1848	5,996	398
1849	7,365	1,369
1850	9,021	1,656
1851	10,982	1,961
1852	12,908	1,926
1853	15,360	2,452
1854	16,720	1,360
1855	18,374	1,054
1856	22,016	3,647
1857	24,503	2,647
1858	26,968	2,465

MILES OF RAILROAD IN UNITED STATES.—*continued.*

Year.	Miles in Operation.	Annual Increase.	Approximate Consumption of Iron and Steel Rails, including Imports. Tons.
1859	28,789	1,821	
1860	30,635	1,846	
1861	31,286	651	
1862	32,120	834	
1863	33,170	1,050	
1864	33,908	738	
1865	35,085	1,177	
1866	36,801	1,742	
1867	39,250	2,449	625,157
1868	42,229	2,979	756,795
1869	46,844	4,615	906,749
1870	52,914	6,070	1,019,153
1871	60,283	7,379	1,341,935
1872	66,171	5,878	1,530,850
1873	70,278	4,107	1,148,849
1874	72,383	1,105	837,724
1875	74,096	1,712	811,960
1876	76,808	2,712	879,916
1877	79,089	2,281	764,744
1878	81,776	2,687	882,695
1879	86,497	4,721	1,157,420
1880	93,671	7,174	1,752,526
1881	104,813	11,142	2,230,421
1882	115,094	10,821	1,912,921
1883	121,494	6,400	1,399,671
1884	125,844	4,350	

The *Railway Age*, of Chicago, places the construction of 1881 at 9,789; 1882, 11,591; 1883, 6,755. It would appear from the table of consumption of rails that 1881 was the year when railroad building was the most active.

In former times "strap rails," consisting of flat pieces of iron $\frac{1}{2}$ to $\frac{5}{8}$ inch thick and from $2\frac{1}{2}$ to $4\frac{1}{2}$ inches wide, were used on all American railroads. A writer in *Brown's History of the First Locomotives in America* says that the track of the Baltimore and Ohio Railroad (about 1830) consisted of cedar cross-pieces and of string pieces of yellow pine from 12 to 24 feet long and 6 inches square, and slightly bevelled upon the top of the upper side for the flange of the wheel, which at that time was upon the outside. On these string-pieces iron rails were placed, and securely nailed down with wrought-iron nails, countersunk in the rail. The company found in practice that the rails would become loosened from the stringers, and that the ends, called "snake heads," would be frequently forced by the wheels through the bottoms of the cars, and cause accidents of a serious nature. The flat rail, however, kept its place in American railroads for many years, and Mr. Poor says: "It was not till 1850 that the longitudinal sill and flat rail was entirely removed from the Utica and Schenectady road, the most important link in the New York Central Line." Flat rails were used on many other roads in the country even after 1860. After the passage of the tariff act in 1842, American capitalists began to consider the advisability of manufacturing iron rails, which had previously been imported free of duty, and in 1845 the first T rails made in the United States were rolled at Danville, Pennsylvania. The T rail is the invention of an American. No steel rails were made in the United States previous to 1867; now no railroad is considered first-class unless it makes use of them.

The aggregate consumption of iron and steel rails is coincident with the periods of heaviest railroad building, averaging for the —

    First period . . . . 690,976 tons per year.
    Second period . . . . 1,189,907 tons per year.
    Third period . . . . 835,408 tons per year.
    Fourth period . . . . 1.690.592 tons per year.

CHAPTER IV.

IMMIGRATION.—1864-1884.

The number of immigrants, according to official figures, arriving in the United States during and including the years 1864 and 1883 was 7,062,670, or one ninth of the total present population of the country.

During the five years from 1864 to 1868 inclusive, there were 1,355,675 arrivals. In the next five years, from 1869 to 1873 inclusive, there were 1,948,823 arrivals. Then followed five years when the immigration fell off over 200,000 per year, as compared with the previous five years, amounting to 893,194, after which came the five "boom" years, when it reached the sum of 2,864,978. The following table will show the immigration for each year and for each period:—

YEARS OF LIGHT IMMIGRATION.

1.	No. of Persons	3.	No. of Persons
1864	193,195	1874	260,814
1865	247,453	1875	191,231
1866	314,917	1876	157,440
1867	310,965	1877	130,502
1868	289,145	1878	153,207
	1,355,675		893,194

YEARS OF HEAVY IMMIGRATION.

2.	No. of Persons	4.	No. of Persons
1869	385,287	1879	250,565
1870	356,303	1880	593,703
1871	346,938	1881	720,045
1872	437,750	1882	730,349
1873	422,545	1883	570,316
	1,948,823		2,864,978

1884 . . . . 454,206 (11 months).

According to the official record, the number of immigrants arriving upon our shores in the year 1881 exceeded the population of the State of Connecticut by 97,345; the population of Maine by 71,109; the population of Nebraska by 267,643; the population of Vermont by 387,759; the population of New Hampshire by 373,054; the population of West Virginia by 101,588, and the population of Rhode Island by 443,514; and it was less only by 127,417 than the aggregate population of the States of Colorado, Delaware, Florida, Nevada, and Oregon. It also exceeded the population of all the Territories of the United States by 113,226, exclusive of the District of Columbia.

This enormous army of workers yearly being landed upon our shores has justly given alarm to European politicians. They do not consist wholly of agricultural laborers, as many suppose, but are composed of all classes, — farmers, mechanics, artisans, and professors, and in a few years, owing to the plasticity of our American institutions, are absorbed into the community, and become active and efficient citizens.

The country which is receiving immigrants and giving them profitable employment is, without doubt, bettering its condition. They not only bring a small capital with them in the shape of actual money, but are, by their labor, necessarily adding to the wealth of the country, in developing its resources, and, by their wants and necessities, are increasing the sales — and consequently the profits — of its traders. If we consider each immigrant as worth to us in labor and money one hundred dollars per year for the first year of his residence, then we received $256,493,200 more in the ten years of heavy immigration than we did in the ten years of light immigration.

"No single cause of dissatisfaction with his home circumstances," says the *New York Shipping and Commercial List* (March 1, 1882), "can be stated, which explains this phenomenal movement of population from the old world to the new. Germany furnishes the largest quota of the tide of immigration, followed by Canada, then by Scandinavia, then by England and Wales, then by Ireland. It might at first glance be thought that militarism would account for the exodus from Germany, but it should be remembered that the French are under a militarism as severe — if not indeed severer — than the Germans, yet France holds her population at home. The birth-rate is high in Germany, and over-population might be regarded as another reason, but in England and Scandinavia the proportion of births to the population is phenomenally low; yet these countries combined sent us nearly as many future citizens as Germany. On any single principle, it is difficult to account for this outflow of population from the old world."

Do we not, however, from the figures heretofore given, gain a verification of the thought, that the causes lie rather here than there? Agreeing as our tables do in their periods of increase and decrease, with like periods in the increase and decrease of failures, and the rise and fall of the price of iron, and the increase and decrease of railroad building, are we not led to reflect that there is a necessary connection between them? And while we may readily believe, from theory, that the personal comfort and advantage of an immigrant would be better subserved in times of commercial activity, we become fixed in that idea when we observe that the immigration of numbers rises and falls in accordance with the varying influence of that force.

From the evidence which we have, we would infer that the emigrant is not flying from evils in his own country, but is rather impelled to try his fortune in this country by the better promise of gain which it from time to time holds out. However, to show the proof of the cause of immigration is not necessary. Our purpose is fulfilled if we have shown that the movement is rhythmical and marked, and on this point the reader will not be likely to disagree. Another fact worthy of notice, but which need not here be justified by figures, being probably within the recollection of each, is, that the number of people visiting foreign lands for pleasure or recreation, and the number of adopted citizens who desire to look once more on the scenes of their childhood, and the number of persons who, having gained a competency, desire to spend the remainder of their days in the land of their birth, rises to large amounts in "good" times, and slowly settles to moderate numbers when the summit of the wave is passed.

CHAPTER V.

STOCKS.

It is but half a century since the first iron railroad was constructed in Massachusetts, from West Stockton to Hudson, a distance of twenty-seven miles. In the first-mentioned town were extensive marble quarries and deposits of iron ore. Nearly all the freight of the western border of the State sought an outlet by way of the Hudson River, and hence the construction of the railroad in question, which was a wonder. About the same time a railroad was built between Albany and Schenectady, and another in eastern Massachusetts. From that small beginning has grown our present system, which, if extended in a single straight line, would reach four times about the globe.

According to Poor's Manual for 1884, the capital, as based on bonds and stocks, is nearly $65,000 per mile. We may safely assert that the entire capitalized debt of all the railroads in the country is considerably over seven billion dollars. The capital so invested enters not only into the operation of our financial institutions, but represents the accumulated savings, in whole or in part, of hundreds of thousands of families.

It is a favorite investment for all classes of society,

both in this country and in Europe, and any fluctuations in its value react upon all classes for weal or woe. It is estimated that in the recent depression of business during the years 1883 and 1884, the capital invested in railroads suffered a depreciation in value sufficient to make — or rather, in this case, to unmake — over one thousand millionaires. Recognizing the fact that this great sum no longer adorns the columns of ledgers, nor figures in the amount of legacies, nor flatters the dreams of avarice, it becomes an interesting task to inquire why it has disappeared, and if we may hope to see it again.

As has been our method in former chapters, let us examine the facts of the case, and see if they present any regular order, or have merely been the footballs of chance. We shall expect, of course, that in the early history of any phenomenon we shall find it to present a course somewhat erratic, and while we would perhaps all agree that the history of every existence is from the simple to the complex, we must remember that it is also from the indefinite to the definite, and from the irregular to the regular. Without stating the reasons which lead us to expect that the history of the New York Stock Market presents such an appearance, we will proceed to make a survey of that history, and leave the truth of the foregoing remarks to be justified by the results.

The following review of the New York Stock Market is from the reports of William B. Dana & Co., publishers of the *Commercial and Financial Chronicle*, and will present a fair conception of the course of prices during that time. This review should be read in connection with the table of yearly highest and lowest prices of stocks, which appears on pages 102, 3 and 4.

"*New York Stock Market, 1860-1885.*

"1860. — In 1860 several of the leading stocks were selling at very low figures. New York & Harlem, in March, sold as low as 8; Michigan Southern at 5, and New York & Erie at 8; Delaware, Lackawanna, & Western, in January, sold at 54. Canton, in December, got down to 14. Cleveland & Pittsburg, in March, down to 5.

"1861-62. — In 1861 the market was generally better; but in 1862 the improvement was more marked. Pennsylvania Coal, and Delaware & Hudson Canal reached 119 in December; Erie, $77\frac{1}{4}$; Harlem, 23; Delaware, Lackawanna, & Western, 130.

"1863. — This year the Harlem Company was authorized to lay tracks on Broadway for horse cars, and the stock reached 179 in August. An injunction prevented the operation. Erie paid its first dividend of $3\frac{1}{2}$ per cent.

"1864. — The Harlem 'corner' culminated in July at 285; that figure, in the same month, being the culminating price of gold. The Harlem corner was the result of large short sales, while nearly the whole of the actual stock had been previously purchased by Commodore Vanderbilt.

Pittsburg, Fort Wayne, & Chicago was in April run up to 152¾. Erie paid two dividends of four per cent each, and Delaware, Lackawanna, & Western, ten per cent in stock, and fifteen in cash.

"1865. — Lee's surrender took place April 9. Erie, in March, 44¼ @ 73¾, and December 91⅝ @ 97. Erie dividends, two of 3½ per cent. Harlem almost entirely neglected. Delaware, Lackawanna, & Western, in January, 222 @ 225; in December, 175. Ohio & Mississippi sold low. Illinois Central paid ten per cent, and varied during the year from 90 @ 138¾.

"1866. — There was a buoyancy in stocks during this year, as it was the first year after the war, when the effects of inflation were apparent; and the movement then commenced in railroad stocks which culminated a few years later in the distribution of the enormous stock dividends which became so notorious. The Milwaukee & St. Paul Railroad was this year formed by bondholders of La Crosse & Milwaukee, and Milwaukee & Prairie du Chien. Commodore Vanderbilt became a prominent stockholder in New York Central Company. Great decline (December) in Pacific Mail Steamship stock; having risen in November to 246, it fell in that month to 170, when sold ex. dividend at 5 per cent cash, and 33⅓ per cent stock, and in December declined to 160.

"1867. — New York Central stock rises from 86⅝ in February, to 123½ in November, — a fact accounted for by continued purchases by the Vanderbilt party. Speculation generally quiet. Express shares admitted on exchange list in October, but by close of year became depressed. Chicago & Alton, on prospects of extra dividends, advanced (December) to $130\frac{1}{2}$. Pacific Mail fell off from 173 in January to $108\frac{1}{4}$ in December — a decline predicted on the advanced condition of its rival, the Union Pacific Railroad. Ohio & Mississippi certificates converted (December) into stock.

"1868. — This year was marked by the contest between the Erie and New York Central companies. Depression in coal shares. Chicago & Alton (September), $158\frac{1}{2}$, and continued high on the prospect of an extra stock dividend. 'Henry Keep corner' in Chicago & Northwestern stock, which rose in October to $97\frac{3}{4}$. 'Vanderbilt corner' in Erie, as against Drew and Fisk, the latter getting the best of it by an issue of convertible bonds, which were immediately exchanged into stock. In November, Fisk cornered Drew in his Erie contracts. The Milwaukee & St. Paul, or 'Garner corner,' in October, carried the price to 111, but proved a failure for the clique. Delaware, Lackawanna, & Western Company leased the Morris & Essex Railroad. New York Central 80 per cent dividend declared in December. Panama paid an extra dividend of 20 per cent stock (September).

"1869. — Stocks generally reached high prices during the first half of the year, the prospect of stock dividends influencing several of the most prominent. Chicago, Rock Island, and Pacific stock advanced (April) to 139, on rumor of extra dividend to represent government land grant. In May the Pacific railroads were opened for business. Erie was struck off the regular stock list for not registering, and not quoted from March to August. Pittsburg, Fort Wayne, & Chicago Railroad was leased to Pennsylvania Railroad Company at 12 per cent on stock, and the stock afterwards increased, and converted thus into a 7 per cent stock. In October the consolidation of the New York Central and the Hudson River railroads was made, and a new distribution of stock certificates issued — 27 per cent on New York Central, and 85 per cent on Hudson River.

"The most important event of the year was the panic of 'Black Friday,' on the 24th of September. This was caused by a great corner in gold, engineered chiefly by Fisk and Gould, and which culminated on Black Friday in a rise of gold to $162\frac{1}{2}$, and an immediate fall to 133 on an announcement that the Government would sell $4,000,000. The clearings of the Gold Exchange Bank became hopelessly involved, the bank suspended, and there was a deadlock for several days. Stocks fell off immensely, and a number of firms suspended.

"1870. — Stocks were generally more quiet in the early months of this year, outsiders having been frightened away by the September (1869) panic. Chicago & Alton stock quoted ex. dividend February 10, the capital stock being increased one third, on terms which made it equivalent to about $33\frac{1}{3}$ cash to stockholders. Panama dividends reduced from 6 per cent quarterly to 6 per cent per annum, owing to competition of Pacific railroads and the taking off steamships on the Pacific Ocean lines.

" 1871. —The stock of the Erie Railway was heavily increased in the four years ending Sept. 30, 1871, by the Fisk and Gould management, so that it stood at $86,536,910, against $25,111,210 in 1867. The price fell in March to $18\frac{7}{8}$, the lowest point touched since 1861. The Chicago fire (October 9) caused a panic in stocks and general business. The Cleveland and Pittsburg Railroad was leased to the Pennsylvania Railroad Company at 10 per cent on capital, afterwards converted by increase into a 7 per cent guaranteed stock. Express stocks rose largely in market value. The 'Woodward Corner' in Chicago & Rock Island, which forced the price up to $130\frac{7}{8}$ in June, was a failure, and resulted disastrously to those engaged in the manœuvre. Lake Shore & Michigan Southern Company (July 27) authorized a new issue equal to 40 per cent of its stock then outstanding, and allotted the same to shareholders on the payment of one third of the par value of the new stock in cash.

" 1872. — The money market worked very closely during most of the year, except from May to September, and at times reached very high figures, interfering seriously with stock operations. James Fisk, Jr., was shot in January. The month of March witnessed the Erie 'revolution,' with the overthrow of the old board of directors and the resignation of Jay Gould as president of the company. Philadelphia & Reading stock was struck from the Exchange Stock list in March, the company refusing compliance with the requirement of registry in New York city. Pacific Mail stock was very active, on the increase by Congress of the company's subsidy to $1,000,000 per year. In September a sharp contest took place between hostile parties in speculation ; and the 17th of that month, when money commanded $\frac{5}{8}$ per cent a day, gold $\frac{5}{8}$ per cent a day, and Erie stock as high as $2\frac{1}{4}$ per cent, was remembered as the day of the 'three corners.' The Boston fire (November 11) caused considerable excitement and depression in stocks. The corner in Chicago & Northwestern in November carried the stock from $77\frac{3}{4}$ to 230.

"1873. — The money market continued very stringent during the early part of the year, and about the 1st of April almost a panic ensued in consequence, as rates for carrying stocks were then quoted as high as $\frac{3}{4}$ to 1 per cent per diem. The summer was noted for a decline of prices and the failure of a number of houses in Wall Street. On the 18th of September Jay Cooke & Co. suspended, and on the 20th the Stock Exchange was closed by order of the Executive Committee, in the height of the panic, and was not opened again till the 30th of that month. The extreme lowest prices in stocks, however, were generally reached early in November, and from that time there was a gradual recovery up to the close of the year. The Erie Railway (February) paid $1\frac{3}{4}$ and (August) 1 per cent, but the stock was not benefited thereby, and continued to decline to the end of the year. In March, Harlem was leased to the New York Central & Hudson River Company at 8 per cent on stock. The Union Pacific was under a cloud in consequence of the Credit Mobilier investigation by Congress.

"1874. — Stocks were less excited, and fluctuated less, than for many years previously. The financial crisis of 1873 had broken up to a considerable extent the strong speculative cliques or combinations which had formerly controlled the market, and had also given the outside public a strong distaste for further ventures in stock speculation. The so-called Granger laws of Wisconsin and other Western States, regulating and reducing the rates for passengers and freights on the railroads within their respective borders, caused much excitement among capitalists and holders of railway securities. The suits brought under the laws were decided against the railroads in the State courts, but were appealed to the United States Supreme Court. Chicago & Northwestern, and Chicago, Milwaukee, & St. Paul, were the stocks chiefly affected by this question. Lake Shore & Michigan Southern was heavily encumbered with floating debt at the beginning, but was able to negotiate bonds to pay it off; and, after passing the August dividend, declared $3\frac{1}{4}$ per cent in December, payable Feb. 1, 1875. Western Union Telegraph began to pay 2 per cent quarterly in July. Erie Railway affairs were much involved. Mr. Watson resigned the presidency, and Mr. Hugh J. Jewett was elected to the office. Pacific Mail was depressed by disasters and dissension among the directors, and by the development that $750,000 had been spent for passing through Congress in 1872 the bill for the $500,000 additional subsidy.

"1875. — The course of prices in 1875 was marked by extreme depression in consequence of the decline in earnings during the first nine months of the year, arising from the depression in commercial affairs and from the low rates caused by sharp competition. Two prominent roads, forming parts of Western trunk lines, defaulted on their interest, and went into the hands of receivers — Erie on the 26th of May, and Toledo, Wabash, & Western, February 22 — and on several other roads belonging to the same general group the net earnings were only sufficient to pay bonded interest. Central Pacific and Union Pacific showed a highly prosperous business, and declared the policy of paying 8 per cent per annum on their stocks. These companies were also greatly strengthened by the United States Supreme Court decision, given November 29, declaring that they are not bound to pay interest on the bonds issued to them by the United States government until the maturity of such bonds. A new line of steamships between China and Japan, the 'Occidental and Oriental,' was established under the auspices of parties interested in the Central Pacific Railroad.

"The grand speculative move of the year was the advance in Union Pacific stock from 36 in January to $79\frac{1}{2}$ in July, and $82\frac{1}{4}$ in November, under the management of

Mr. Jay Gould and other parties, mostly in Boston. Second to the advance in Union Pacific, the most extraordinary fluctuation in any stock was that in Pacific of Missouri, which sold at 55 in April and $47\frac{5}{8}$ in September, and went to $7\frac{1}{2}$ in October. This extraordinary break in the stock of a road leased at fixed annual dividends (to the Atlantic & Pacific) was demoralizing in its effects, and tended to increase the lack of confidence in values.

"1876. — The year 1876 was one of great depression in values. The first serious check came in the shape of the railroad freight war, which commenced in the latter part of April, — a move on the part of Commodore Vanderbilt, as president of the New York Central and Lake Shore companies, to secure one uniform rate for through freights from competitive points at the West over any of the four leading trunk lines to the Atlantic seaboard. Freights were reduced to 20 cents per 100 pounds from Chicago to New York, and the war was not settled till December 16, when an agreement was made that produce shipped by rail to the seaboard, intended for export, should be charged at one rate to any of the three cities, New York, Philadelphia, or Baltimore, while that shipped for home consumption should have the benefit of a lower rate to the two cities last named. Second to the depressing influence arising from the railroad war, the break-up in the anthracite coal combination, and the consequent decline in stocks of the coal-carrying roads, was the chief event of importance. As usual under such circumstances, the bears in stocks made the most of these discouraging features to hammer the market to their utmost, and thus added to the gloomy feeling prevalent. New York Central & Hudson River held its own until the last of the year, when the critical illness of Mr. Vanderbilt, together with the issue of the company's report for the year ending September 30, affected the stock unfavorably. Erie changed but little, and the bondholders' committee in London were still engaged at the end of the year in endeavoring to carry out the proposed plan of settlement. Ohio & Mississippi went into the hands of Messrs. Torrance & King, as receivers, on November 17. Illinois Central stock declined heavily from decreased earnings on the road, and the company declared only 2 per cent dividend, payable Feb. 1, 1877. Lake Shore, through an enormous economy of expenditures, declared 2 per cent in July, and $1\frac{1}{2}$ for the last six months of the year. Pacific of Missouri was foreclosed under the third mortgage. Railroad earnings in the first half of the year made a remarkably good exhibit, and out of thirty-two roads whose reports of gross earnings for the six months ending June 30, 1876, were published in the *Chronicle*, all but five showed an increase as compared with the same time in 1875. In the latter half of the year gross earnings fell off materially, in consequence of the small crops, and, with the low rates for freight established by the railroad war, the net profits from operations were reduced proportionately more than the gross receipts.

" 1877. — The first half of the year 1877 was a period

of extreme depression in the New York stock market. There was no panic, and no violent or extraordinary events to suddenly break down the market, but values shrunk away steadily under the unfavorable circumstances affecting stocks, assisted by the most persistent and vigorous hammering by a strong combination of bear operations. Commodore Vanderbilt died early in January, and in March the trunk-line agreement of December 16, 1876, — 'one rate to the seaboard,' — for which he had contended so vigorously, was abandoned, and the unsettled condition of affairs among the trunk lines, after the ruinous strife between them for the previous twelve months, was exceedingly discouraging. Only second to the trunk-line difficulty, and still more remediless, was the trouble among the coal-carrying and mining companies, arising from the low price of coal. The Central Railroad of New Jersey went into the hands of a receiver in February. The Philadelphia & Reading Company was obliged to obtain concessions from its creditors, and the two prominent New York companies — the Delaware, Lackawanna, & Western Railroad and the Delaware & Hudson Canal Company — saddled with burdensome leases, resorted to new mortgage loans to meet their current obligations.

"In June the trunk-line companies made a new agreement for freight rates, based on mileage; the two leading coal-carrying companies had negotiated loans which placed them beyond the danger of present embarrassment; the reports of a very abundant harvest began to come in after the middle of July ; the telegraph consolidation was under negotiation, and finally completed in August; and there was now formed (in July) a very strong speculative combination to put up stocks. The upward movement was delayed temporarily by the serious riots at Pittsburg and throughout the country, caused by the railroad strikes ; but as soon as these ended, in the early part of August, the advance began in earnest, and stocks were carried up largely. Railroad earnings began to increase in August, and during the autumn months the principal grain-carrying roads showed a large improvement over their earnings for the same time in 1876. The principal circumstances affecting railroad earnings in the year 1877 were as follows : 1. The exceedingly low rates on the trunk lines during the greater part of the year, and a moderate decrease in the volume of business on those lines. 2. The diminished crops of 1876 in the West and Northwest, leaving a small volume of freight for the railroads in the first half of 1877, which had to be carried at low rates in consequence of the 'Granger' decisions against the railroads, and the sharp competition for business. 3. The exceptional prosperity and increasing population in northern Texas, Arkansas, and Missouri, which helped the railroads running into those sections. 4. The steady business on the main line of the Pacific railroads. 5. The great crops of 1877, which changed the entire situation when they began to come to market. 6. The agreements among trunk lines, both Western and Southwestern, which were made in the fall for the maintenance of better rates for freight.

"1878. — In the early months of 1878 there was much dullness in stocks, and prices were comparatively low. During the second quarter there was much more animation, and prices made a considerable advance up to and including the month of July, when high figures were reached. Both the prominent railroad companies of the Northwest — the Chicago & Northwestern, and the Chicago, Milwaukee, & St. Paul — paid dividends on their preferred stock, and the first-named on its common stock, and all the principal grain-carrying roads showed earnings far in excess of the first six months of 1877. In July and August it became apparent that there had been some damage to the wheat crop in the Northwestern States, and the stocks of the companies just named fell off very sharply to the lowest prices of the year. In regard to the trunk-line railroads between the seaboard and the West, the important movement of the year was in the election of Mr. William H. Vanderbilt as president of the Michigan Central Railroad, which, with his control of the Lake Shore and the Canada Southern, placed under his management every line from Chicago eastward, north of the Pennsylvania Railroad's leased lines, and left the Canada roads without western connections. An important conference of railroad officials was held at Saratoga in August, in which Mr. Vanderbilt was understood as clearly favoring a policy of harmonious working among the several lines in their adjustment of freight and passenger rates.

"The combination among the anthracite coal-mining

and carrying corporations was maintained through the year, and served to keep up the prices of their stocks; but coal business was unsatisfactory, and the combination was not renewed for 1879, owing to the objections of the Lehigh Valley operators, and prices of stocks fell off sharply in December. The business in railroad bonds in the last quarter of the year was large beyond precedent, and much of it on speculative account. The Central Railroad of New Jersey re-organization scheme was carried out by the re-adjustment of its securities. The Erie Railway was sold under foreclosure of the second consolidated mortgage, April 24, and bought in by trustees representing the English reorganization committee. The Canada Southern bonds were guaranteed as to interest by the New York Central & Hudson River Railroad Company, and the stock, which had been practically valueless, sold in December at $45\frac{1}{2}$.

"1879. — For five years the painful process of foreclosure, settlement, and reorganization was steadily going on, and in 1877 and 1878 the railroads were greatly assisted by the heavy tonnage arising from the large crops, until at length, in 1879, the idea dawned upon investors, speculators, and capitalists that the railroads were not really the worthless properties that they had seemed to be. Then there was a rush to purchase low-priced stocks and bonds, such as had never been seen before, and the advance in prices was marvellous.

"One of the leading events of the year was the Gould

and Field combination, announced in April, by which the St. Louis, Kansas City, & Northern, and the Wabash railways were to be consolidated as one line, and, building an extension to Omaha, formed one line from Kansas City and Omaha in the West to Toledo at the East. Mr. Gould already had the control of Union Pacific and Kansas Pacific, and purchased afterwards a control in the Missouri Pacific and Denver & Rio Grande, together with a number of minor roads, and in these heavy investments of capital he changed his position from that of a stock operator to that of a railroad capitalist and manager. In the first half of the year the greatest activity at the Stock Exchange was in January, April, and May, but after the middle of July, with the prospect of very heavy crops, there was another bound in prices, which went on with few interruptions until the culmination in November, and the sharp break in prices which reached the extreme point on the 21st of that month. In October and early in November the excitement was intense, and the transactions at the Stock Exchange were so large that it was quite impossible to report all the sales. After the heavy decline just referred to, in which many small speculators were crippled, the market showed no great animation during the balance of the year. A transaction which excited no less interest than the St. Louis, Wabash, & Pacific consolidation was the sale by Mr. William H. Vanderbilt, in November, of 250,000 shares of New York Central & Hudson stock at 120 to a syndicate composed of Messrs. J. S. Morgan & Co. of London, Jay Gould, and others.

The Western Union Telegraph declared a scrip dividend of 17 per cent in June. The new American Union Telegraph, under the control of Mr. Jay Gould made much progress in establishing its lines on leading railroad routes. The Chicago & Alton built a new line to Kansas City. The St. Paul and Northwest companies added largely to their mileage by the purchase and construction of new lines. The Missouri, Kansas, & Texas stock and bonds were among the most active, in consequence of pending negotiations for a lease to the Chicago, Burlington, & Quincy. The reorganized Erie stocks, under the name of New York, Lake Erie, & Western, first appeared August 22. The St. Louis & San Francisco Railroad securities were high and active under the negotiations with the Atchison, Topeka, & Santa Fé for a through line to the Pacific. A contract was also made in December for extending the Texas & Pacific to the Pacific coast.

"1880. — The stock exchanges were centres of interest in the year 1880 to a degree never before witnessed. The price of seats in the New York Stock Exchange rose to about $25,000 in December. The total reported sales of shares at the board amounted in round figures to 97,000,000, against 74,000,000 in 1879, and the sales of railroad bonds to $570,000,000 against $412,000,000 in 1879. The great number of new stocks and bonds admitted to the Stock Exchange list was one of the notable features. So great were the combinations, consolidations, and extensions of railroads in the year, that the analogy as to the course of stocks with former periods was lost, and comparisons of earnings or prices with prior years were rendered of little value. Thus, what was the worth of a comparison of 1880 with 1879 on Louisville & Nashville stock, doubled in amount, and the company operating 700 miles more of road; on Wabash, St. Louis, & Pacific consolidated; on Union Pacific, embracing the former Kansas Pacific, and other bankrupt roads; on St. Paul, with mileage increased 1,300 miles; on Northwest, with 300 miles more of road; on Rock Island, with its double stock? The year 1880 was one *sui generis* in the stock market, and must stand alone. The speculator or investor who took the experience of former years as his guide frequently lost money.

"But, notwithstanding the general strength of the situation, based upon the immense income of the railroad corporations, the year was not all smooth in the stock market, and in May and June came a depression of extraordinary severity. Indeed, there has seldom been a worse decline in the stock market, arising from what seemed to be purely speculative influences. There was no panic, no failures of consequence among bankers or stock-brokers, but a gradual and irresistible shrinkage in prices, under heavy and continuous sales, which carried down the whole list 10, 20, 30 per cent from the highest made in the early months of the year. The shock to outside operators was great, and although there was a partial recovery of tone in prices in June and following months, the general market did not again show a decided activity and buoyancy until after the elections on the 12th of October. From that time until the end of the year everything was on the upward move, and even the tight money of early December was insufficient to produce any considerable break in prices. Bears in stocks habitually lost money, except in Western Union Telegraph, which collapsed to $77\frac{1}{2}$ on December 17, from $104\frac{7}{8}$ on November 22.

"Noting the leading events of the year in the order of their occurrence, we find that in January the New York Central & Hudson syndicate availed themselves of their option to take 100,000 shares more of stock from Mr. Vanderbilt; the consolidation of the Union Pacific, the Kansas Pacific, and the Denver, South Park, & Pacific Railroad companies was made; the Missouri, Kansas, & Texas Railroad was obtained by Mr. Jay Gould; the Louisville & Nashville purchased control of the stock of the Nashville, Chattanooga, & St. Louis Railroad; the sale was made by the Huntington party of $10,000,000 Central Pacific stock to a syndicate of bankers; in April, the stock of the Chicago, Burlington, & Quincy Railroad sold ex. 20 per cent stock dividend, made on the consolidation with Burlington & Missouri in Nebraska.

"The next event of striking interest was the suspension in May of the Philadelphia & Reading Railroad and its coal company, and the appointment of receivers on May 24. In June the Rock Island Railroad Company formed a consolidation, and made a 100 per cent dividend to stockholders. In August a contest began between the

Chicago, Burlington, & Quincy, and the Wabash, St. Louis, & Pacific railroads as to the control of Western lines, which was finally settled in October. The Louisville & Nashville Railroad declared its 100 per cent stock dividend, payable December 1. Mr. Jay Gould, owning a controlling interest in the stock of the Missouri Pacific Railroad, made a consolidation in August, with provision for issuing $30,000,000 stock and $30,000,000 bonds. He also purchased in November most of the stock of the Denver, South Park, & Pacific Road, and in December a large block of St. Louis & Iron Mountain stock, and a majority of International & Great Northern stock. The Western Union Telegraph quarterly statement of receipts was published December 8, showing a large decrease, and the stock fell off heavily.

"1881. — The Stock Exchange in New York and other cities absorbed more than the usual attention, as centres of a constantly growing financial business, in which the whole community was more or less interested. At the New York Board the price of seats advanced in the first half of the year to over $30,000, but fell off again in the latter part of the year, when commission business was less profitable. It was notable that the first six months of the year had much the larger business, and for the whole year there was an increase in stocks, but a decrease in railroad bonds. The total sales of all stocks were, in round figures, 113,000,000 shares, against 97,000,000 in 1880, and 74,000,000 in 1879. The sales of railroad bonds amounted to $387,000,-

000, against $570,000,000 in 1880, and $412,000,000 in 1879.

"Although the year 1881 witnessed the most wonderful consolidations, stock-waterings, and other enormous issues of stocks and bonds, it may fairly be said that the year passed without a single collapse of importance in the market, and without any depression which amounted to a stock panic. There was no break, even, which could be compared to that of November, 1879, or May, 1880, and this, too, notwithstanding such occurrences as the money pressure of February 25, when loans cost one per cent a day, and the assassination of President Garfield on July 2, when the country was shocked to its foundation. The great strength of the leading operators, who were interested in sustaining the market, and the general confidence in the prosperity of the country, which caused a quick rally from every decline, were simply astonishing.

"In looking at the controlling influences of the year, we find that the winter opened with great severity, and in the Northwest the obstructions to railroad traffic had hardly ceased by the first of May. After the hard winter came the partial failure of crops and the great drought throughout the West, which inflicted a further loss of business in the later months of the year. On the other hand, the movements of passengers and general merchandise, including the transportation of material for about 9,000 miles of new railroad, were so large, that the Western railroads kept up their gross earnings quite remarkably, and in many cases showed a considerable increase over 1880. In the last half of the year came the railroad war among the trunk lines, by which the rates between the West and the seaboard were so reduced that the transportation between Chicago and New York was done at prices barely paying expenses.

"At the Stock Exchange the year opened with buoyancy, under the influences of the manipulations of Western Union Telegraph stock by Mr. Gould, which was advanced to high prices on the consolidation of the company with the American Union and Atlantic & Pacific, and the distribution of $38\frac{1}{4}$ per cent as a stock dividend. There was afterward no great feature until the end of February, when the contraction caused by the action of the banks in apprehension of the passage of the funding law with the 'Carlisle' amendment, caused a money panic for a few days, and produced a very sharp decline in stocks on the 25th of February. There was speedy recovery from this as soon as money relaxed, and the confidence in stocks quickly reasserted itself. Except the ordinary fluctuations of the market, there was nothing of great importance from this time forward until the shooting of President Garfield on July 2, which caused a temporary decline; but as the next two days (Sunday and July 4) were business holidays, the time given for reflection was sufficient to make a steadier feeling, and with a strong support at the opening on July 5, it was soon shown that the danger of a panic was gone.

"In the last half of the year there occurred only the usual variations of the stock market until December, when the effect of the long-continued war in rates, together with a growing interest on the bear side, led to a gradual decline. The first decline was precipitated by a sharp fall in Denver & Rio Grande stock, under the attacks, as reported, of Mr. Gould, and soon after came the reports of the Vanderbilt roads, showing a heavy loss in net earnings, which were followed, on December 30, by the reported troubles in Wabash, and the passing of its January dividend on preferred stock; and under all these influences the market closed with much depression, and with many stocks near the lowest prices of the year.

"1882. — The stock market in 1882 showed a trifle less activity in the volume of business transacted than in the previous year. In taking a general view of the course of prices, it is found that there were three periods of considerable depression, and only in July and August was there genuine buoyancy in stocks caused by outside purchases, uninfluenced by speculative manipulation or the manœuvres of professional operators.

"After showing some strength and animation in the early part of the year, the market collapsed and ran into a condition of great weakness, which culminated in the lowest prices about the 23d of February. From this there was some recovery, as negotiations progressed for the settlement of the trunk-line war, and the market went on in a feverish condition, with frequent fluctuations, until the early part of March, when weakness again set in ; and from the 10th to the 13th there was a feeling of increasing gloominess, and a large amount of stocks was thrown overboard. On the latter day Mr. Gould made his famous exhibit at his office, to a few of his influential friends, of a large amount of his stocks and bonds, to prove that he was in no straits for money, as some of the bear rumors had reported. According to the accounts Mr. Gould produced a strong box from which he took a large number of stock certificates, including $23,000,000 of Western Union, $12,000,000 of Missouri Pacific, $6,000,000 of Manhattan Elevated, $2,000,000 of Wabash common, and $10,000,000 of bonds of the New York and Metropolitan railways and Wabash preferred stock. He also offered to show some $30,000,000 of railroad bonds, but the gentlemen were satisfied.

"When the result of the harvest was pretty well known in July, there began a genuine and active purchasing movement, and the interest of the public in the market was larger than it had been in a long time. This strength was continued, with some variations, through August, but in September there was a check put on the advancing tendency, and it was generally believed that Mr. Gould was then opposing any further rise in the market, although his interests forbade that he should become a decided bear on prices The stringency in money afterward assisted the bear interest, and this was followed by the railroad w: .· among the companies of the Northwest, so that fro ;

September to December — when this railroad war was settled — there was never a time that the stock market presented a strong and healthy outlook calculated to invite the investment of new money, and much of that time the depression of the stock exchange was so severe that prices of a number of stocks reached the lowest point made in several years.

"The Northwestern railroad war was finally settled about December 15, and in consequence of that, the tone decidedly improved, and, without any great activity, the better feeling was maintained, with some exceptions, till the close of the year.

"Any account of the stock market in 1882 would be quite incomplete which did not refer to the large and rapid decline in a few of the highly speculative stocks, such as Denver & Rio Grande, Richmond & Danville, Richmond & West Point, Louisville & Nashville, and Hannibal & St. Joseph. The break in the Hannibal & St. Joseph stocks was the result of the corner of the previous year, while the Richmond & Danville stocks were so closely held that they labored under the same disadvantage. The weak point in Louisville & Nashville was its large funded and floating debt. Denver & Rio Grande was perhaps weakest of all, partly because of increased competition, but mainly because of the additions to its stock and debt.

"The combination and consolidation of leading lines of railroad continued in 1882. In January the Atchison,

Topeka, & Santa Fe, and the St. Louis & San Francisco lost their control of the Atlantic & Pacific Road, which was under construction, and Messrs. C. P. Huntington and Jay Gould entered the directory of the Atlantic & Pacific. Great Western and Grand Trunk of Canada were consolidated under one management. The Erie road, in April, made permanent its connections with Cincinnati by getting control of a majority of the stock of the Cincinnati, Hamilton, & Dayton company. In July, the Rock Island obtained possession of the Minneapolis & St. Louis, and the Chicago, Burlington, & Quincy opened its extension to Denver. In September the Delaware, Lackawanna, & Western leased the Buffalo extension, giving it a Lake Erie outlet for its coal, and forming another through route from New York to the West. But the most striking event of the year in railroad negotiations was the purchase of a controlling interest in the stock of the New York, Chicago, & St. Louis road (capital $50,000,000), by parties in the interest of the Lake Shore & Michigan Southern, and the Cleveland, Columbus, Cincinnati, & Indianapolis, the Messrs. Vanderbilt being most prominent among the purchasers. The Michigan Central leased the Canada Southern, making a further consolidation in the same interests; and in December it was announced that the Messrs. Vanderbilt and others identified with the Chicago & Northwestern management had purchased a controlling interest in the stock of the Chicago, St. Paul, Minneapolis, & Omaha road.

"1883. — In the stock market the decline in prices during the year 1883 was more general and more severe than in any prior year since the gloomy period of 1873–1878. To account for this extreme depression, it is necessary to go back a few years and take an observation of the actual condition of railroad affairs. The building of many new railroads, and the consolidations and combinations which took place among a great number of the old companies, led to the floating of a mass of new stocks and bonds, upon which it was found impossible to earn interest or dividends. This speculative stuff was floated during the general activity, commonly designated as the 'boom,' which lasted, with more or less variation, from July 1, 1878, to July 1, 1881. Railroad stocks or income bonds, which have no reasonable prospect of dividends for four or five years to come, are not often worth more than 20 to 25 in the market, and some of them may be worth much less. Hence, if the market is loaded up with a mass of such securities at prices ranging from 40 to 100, it is plainly in a dangerous condition, where a great shrinkage in values may begin at any time. The law is almost sure to assert itself in time, and after holders have become convinced that there is no hope of making anything by a rise in prices, or, still worse, that there is no hope of getting rid of their burden for the price at which they took it, the effort to unload will begin, and will keep on till liquidation has taken place.

"These remarks are necessary to an understanding of

the stock market of 1883. The public had become loaded with securities which gave no prospect of furnishing income. They did not realize this fully till 1882 and 1883, and then they began to unload.

"Railroad traffic and earnings were large beyond precedent. While other branches of business were languishing, and while even railroad stocks were declining severely at the stock exchanges, the railroads were showing a heavy business, and reporting the largest earnings ever made. The year 1883 was plainly the maximum year yet reached in railroad business. The decline in stocks, therefore, arose more from the immediate influences bearing upon the markets, and from apprehension as to the future, than from any weakness actually developed in the railroad situation. But tonnage in 1883 was very heavy from the large crops of 1882; from general activity in the movements of various classes of merchandise; from a heavy coal tonnage; from an early movement of crops to market in the fall of 1883, and from a large immigration and settlement of new lands at the West. Passenger business was also heavy. Sharp competition, however, began to develop in consequence of the opening of many new lines; the Iowa pool rupture was barely healed; and at the close of 1883 the signs were generally unfavorable for a continuance of the great railroad prosperity which had been so conspicuous during that year.

"As the year progressed, the market went from bad to worse, and the climax of depression was reached after the default of the Ohio Central Railroad, on September 1, and the great break in the Northern Pacific and Oregon & Trans-Continental stocks, after the last spike (golden spike) was driven, completing the main line of the Northern Pacific, on the 8th day of September. Railroad earnings were almost abnormally large, and on many roads the gross receipts were the largest ever made, owing to the very heavy tonnage at high rates. Among the leading events of the year were the leasing of the Central Railroad of New Jersey, from June 1, to the Philadelphia & Reading; the lease of the New York, Pennsylvania, & Ohio, from May 1, by the New York, Lake Erie, & Western; the strike of the Western Union Telegraph operators in July, and the breaking up of the Iowa pool in December. Prices at the end of December were generally near to the lowest point of the year."

"1884. — The stock market opened in January with depression, which was brought over from December. On the first of the year a receiver was appointed for the New York & New England Railroad, and a break in West Shore bonds and appointment of a receiver for the North River Construction Company, together with a new break in Oregon & Trans-Continental and the Northern Pacifics, caused a gloomy feeling in the market. On the 26th of the month a turn was given by the formation of a syndicate which made a loan to the Oregon & Trans-Continental on the pledge of its stocks, and thereafter a quick move against the shorts was made, which caused a sharp advance in prices, and a firm tone during the balance of the month and throughout most of February, when the speculative support kept up prices till near the end of that month. On the first of March the corner in Delaware, Lackawanna, and Western took place, which carried the price up to $133\frac{1}{8}$, regular, and $139\frac{1}{2}$ for cash. This was demoralizing to the bears, and about the middle of the month another squeeze in New York Central to 122 increased the feeling. Under the influence of these corners there was a chance for the large stock speculators to get off a considerable amount of stock, and, with some fluctuations, there was a declining tendency till the end of April."

On the 14th of May came the panic, which the *Commercial and Financial Chronicle* referred to, in its financial review of that month, substantially as follows: —

" This was the culminating point in a period of nearly eleven years, during which had occurred the slow recovery from the crash of 1873, the rise and development of the most gigantic speculation in railroads that any country had ever seen, and finally the inevitable downward movement continued during nearly three years, from July, 1881, and ending in May, 1884, with what came near to being a serious financial crisis. At the end of three years of unparalleled shrinkage in stock-exchange values, the crash was at last precipitated by the turning up of a line of frauds in financial operations which had hardly been matched before; and the worst and heaviest of these was perpetrated under the influence of the name (though not with the personal connivance) of that distinguished soldier and President, General U. S. Grant. The names of Fish, of the Marine Bank, Grant & Ward, John C. Eno, and a few others, must be woven into the history of May, 1884.

"The Marine Bank and Grant & Ward suspended on Tuesday, May 6, and the following week the Metropolitan Bank suspended, followed by a number of banker and broker firms, and the height of the excitement was reached. The Clearing House banks joined to support each other by issuing 'Clearing House certificates,' by which means the Metropolitan Bank was enabled to resume on Thursday, May 15, the day after its suspension. The Second National Bank was robbed of about $3,000,000 by the stock speculations of its president, John C. Eno, but this deficiency was immediately made good by the father of the defaulter and other directors."

The greatest depression in tone and in the prices of many stocks was reached about Friday, June 27, when the unmitigated bear attacks on the market led to such an overselling that there was a very quick rally the next day, and a semi-panic among the bears. After the first of July and the occurrence of very few defaults by railroads, there was a wonderful recovery in tone, and an improvement in prices, from which there was never afterwards a relapse to the panicky feeling of May and June. The upward movement in stocks was pushed in July and August, with the assistance of different pools, which of course sold out and left the market in a languishing condition by the first of September. In the last four months of the year the benefit of the large crop movement was greatly counteracted by the disagreement among the railroads and cutting of rates, and by the bad condition of the anthracite coal trade, the default of Reading, and especially by the long-continued contest between the West Shore road and the New York Central & Hudson over passenger rates. From the termination of the Presidential election excitement, late in November, till the end of the year, there never was a hearty bull movement in stocks. It had been generally accepted for some months that Mr. Vanderbilt was practically a bear on the situation, and had sold a large amount of his stocks, and on December 12th the Lackawanna pool closed out their holdings, so that there was no strong support left to the market, and prices closed at the end of the year with great depression.

Some of the principal events of the year, bearing directly on the stock market, were as follows : On January 1, a meeting of the directors of the New York & New England Railroad was held in Hartford, and on their application President Clark was appointed receiver at two o'clock on the morning of January 2. The North River Construction Company, building the New York, West Shore, & Buffalo Railroad was in difficulties, and ex-Judge Ashbel Green was appointed receiver, January 12. In the latter part of May, the directors of the New York, Lake Erie, & Western Railroad decided to pass the interest, due June 1, on the second consolidated bonds. On May 28, Messrs. Solon Humphreys, of New York, and Thomas E. Tutt, of St. Louis, were appointed receivers of the Wabash, St. Louis, & Pacific Railroad. On June 2 the directors of the Philadelphia & Reading Railroad, and Philadelphia & Reading Coal & Iron Company, applied to the United States Circuit Court to have receivers appointed, and Edwin M. Lewis, George B. de Keim, the president, and Stephen A. Caldwell were so appointed. On June 7, the New York, West Shore, & Buffalo Railroad was placed in the hands of ex-Judge Horace Russell and Theodore Houston as receivers, and on July 1, default was made on the first mortgage bonds. In June, the Union Pacific suspended dividends, and a radical change was made in the management of the road, Mr. Charles Francis Adams, Jr., being elected president in place of Mr. Sidney Dillon. The dividends usually declared in June and payable in August were passed on Michigan Central and Canada Southern, and the quarterly dividend of Lake Shore was reduced from 2 to $1\frac{1}{2}$ per cent and in December the dividend was passed. The Central Pacific passed its dividends, the last paid being that of February 1, at 3 per cent. The usual quarterly dividend on New York Central, payable in October, was reduced from 2 to $1\frac{1}{2}$ per cent, and soon after the company announced that $10,000,000 5 per cent debenture bonds had been issued. On November 1 default was made on Denver & Rio Grande first mortgages, and Chicago & Atlantic firsts. In November an important change was made in the board of directors of the New York, Lake Erie, & Western Railroad, and Mr. John King was elected president in place of Mr. Hugh J. Jewett, who retired from the management of the company.

While we do not agree, in many instances, with the writer of this review, in respect to the causes of the frequent fluctuations — they being so numerous and hidden as to defy the labor of research — yet the points mentioned are to be taken into consideration in forming a conception of the course through which the prices have passed.

The ten stocks whose yearly range of price is given on pages 102–104 were taken at random. One is the stock of a steamship company, now having routes upon the Atlantic and Pacific oceans, extending to points as far distant as New York, Panama, San Francisco, Washington Territory, China, Australia, the Hawaiian Islands, Mexico, and Central America. Two — the Delaware and Hudson Canal Company, and the Delaware, Lackwanna, and Western Railroad Company — are chiefly engaged as coal miners and carriers. Of the remainder, one is a short road across the Isthmus of Panama, and six are trunk lines whose tracks cover many prosperous States and Territories. The average mean price of the ten stocks was obtained by taking the mean between the highest and lowest price of each stock for each year, adding them together, and dividing by ten. We determine the average yearly range by taking the range from highest to lowest of each stock, for each year, adding them together and dividing the sum by ten.

NAME OF PROPERTY.	1860.	1861.	1862.	1863.	1864.	1865.	1866.	1867.
	L. H.	L. H.	L. H.	L. H.	L. H.	L. H.	L. H.	L. H.
Del. and Hudson Canal Co.	80, 101½	80, 92	84¼, 119	118, 179½	152, 247	130, 215	133, 160	139, 155
Pacific Mail Steamship Co.	74, 107	50, 109	91, 137	136¼, 239½	214, 320	151, 329	160, 246	117, 173
New York Central R. R. Co.	69, 92½	68, 88	79⅝, 107¾	107, 140	109, 145	80, 119	86⅜, 123½	94¼, 118½
Erie R.R. Co.	8, 39	17, 88	31⅜, 65¼	66, 122	82, 126	44¼, 98½	55½, 97	52, 77½
Michigan Central R. R. Co.	35, 73½	40, 111	47, 93	91, 128¾	114½, 157	90½, 118¼	100¾, 117¾	102, 112¾
Michigan Southern R. R. Co.	5, 25	10¾, 106	19, 47	M.S. & N.I. 45⅝, 113	57, 118⅝	MICH. S. 49¾, 84½	66½, 101	64⅝, 86½
Panama R. R. Co.	106, 146½	99, 121	110, 170	171, 200	200, 300	200, 270	235, 270	254, 312
Chicago and Rock Island R. R. Co.	42½, 84¼	30¾, 118	50, 85½	82¼, 123½	95, 149⅜	81¾, 113½	91, 123¼	85, 104
Chicago, Burlington, and Quincy R. R. Co. . .	40, 92¾	51, 98½	57, 119	99, 131	111, 149	100, 130	109¼, 138¾	124, 150
Del. and Lackawanna R. R. Co.	54, 96	68, 91½	80, 130	130, 198	195, 265	175, 225	124, 162½	109¾, 130
AVERAGE FLUCTUATION PER YEAR	34½	50⅞	42½	53	63¾	50	37¾	27¾
AVERAGE MEAN PRICE OF TEN PROPERTIES .	68⅞	76⅞	86⅛	131	165⅜	140	135	128

Name of Property.	1868.	1869.	1870.	1871.	1872.	1873.	1874.	1875.
	L. H.	L. H.	L. H.	L. H.	L. H.	L. H.	L. H.	L. H.
Del. and Hudson Canal Co.	119½, 165	120, 134	115½, 127	115, 125	115, 124	99, 120	113, 121	110¼, 124
Pacific Mail Steamship Co.	86, 120⅜	42, 123⅝	30⅞, 46½	39½, 58½	53⅝, 103¼	25, 76⅞	33⅝, 51½	31⅞, 45⅞
New York Central R. R. Co.	110¼, 159⅝	153, 217⅞	N.Y.C.& H.R. 86, 102	84¼, 103⅝	89, 101⅞	77⅞, 106½	95⅞, 105⅝	100, 107⅜
Erie R. R. Co.	35½, 81⅝	21, 42	20½, 28¼	18⅞, 35	30, 75⅞	35⅝, 69¼	26, 51¼	12¼, 35½
Michigan Central R. R. Co.	106⅞, 129	114, 136¾	116, 126	114, 126	113, 120	65, 108¼	68½, 95½	53, 82¼
Michigan Southern R. R. Co.	80, 94	L.S. & M.S. 81¼, 109¾	84, 100½	85½, 116¼	83½, 98¼	70⅞, 96⅝	67⅞, 84⅝	51¼, 80⅛
Panama R. R. Co. . . .	290, 369	163, 348	72, 170	49, 75	72, 148¾	80, 130	101, 118	110⅝, 172
Chicago and Rock Island R. R. Co.	85, 118	101⅞, 139	101⅜, 126	94, 130⅞	101, 118⅛	63, 117⅜	92½, 109⅛	100½, 109⅜
Chicago, Burlington, and Quincy R. R. Co. . .	138, 175	147, 200	145½, 162	125, 160	127½, 143	78, 120	97, 112	103¼, 119
Del., Lackawanna and Western R. R. Co. . .	110, 131	105¼, 120½	100½, 112½	102, 111½	91, 112½	79½, 106	99, 112⅜	106½, 123
Average Fluctuation per Year	37⅛	51½	22⅞	21½	26½	37½	16⅝	22
Average Mean Price of Ten Properties .	135⅛	131	98⅝	94	101	86¼	87¾	88⅞

Name of Property.	1876.	1877.	1878.	1879.	1880.	1881.	1882.	1883.	1884.
	L. H.	L. H.	L. H.	L. H.	L. H.	L. H.	L. H.	L. H.	L. H.
Del. and Hudson Canal Co.	61¼, 125	25½, 74½	34⅜, 55	38, 89⅛	60, 92¾	89⅝, 115¼	102¾, 119¾	102½, 112⅛	67, 114
Pacific Mail Steamship Co.	16¼, 39⅞	12⅞, 26¼	12½, 23⅜	10⅝, 39½	27½, 62	39, 62¼	34½, 48¾	28, 44¾	31, 57⅛
New York Central and Hudson R. R. . . .	96, 117½	85¼, 109¼	103¾, 115	112, 139	122, 155⅜	130¼, 155	123⅝, 138	111½, 129⅛	83½, 122
Erie Common R. R. . .	7¾, 23⅜	4⅝, 15	4 assess. pd. 17⅛, 22½	21⅛, 49	30, 51⅛	39¾, 52⅞	33¼, 43⅝	26⅞, 39¼	11⅛, 28⅜
Michigan Central R. R. Co.	34⅝, 65½	35⅝, 74¼	58½, 75	73¾, 98	75, 130⅛	84¾, 126½	77, 103⅞	77, 100⅛	51¾, 94½
Lake Shore and Mich. Southern R. R. Co. . .	48¾, 68⅝	45, 73⅜	55⅞, 71⅝	67, 108	95, 139⅝	Ctfs. 112⅝, 135¾	98, 120⅛	92¾, 114⅞	59½, 104¾
Panama R. R. Co. . . .	122, 140	80, 130	112, 131	123, 182	168, 225	190, 200	165, 204	100, 100	No quotation
Chicago, Rock Island, and Pacific R. R. Co. .	98⅜, 111⅝	82½, 105½	98, 122	119, 150½	100, 143	129, 148⅝	122, 140¼	116½, 127¼	100¼, 126¾
Chicago, Burlington, and Quincy R. R. Co. . .	112½, 121½	94, 118⅞	99¼, 114⅞	111⅛, 134½	120, 183*	133½, 182½	120½, 141	115¾, 129⅜	107, 127¾
Del., Lackawanna, and Western R. R. Co. . .	64½, 120⅜	30⅞, 77	41, 61⅞	43, 94	68½, 110¼	107, 129¼	116¼, 150	111½, 131½	86¾, 132½
Average Fluctuation per Year	27	30½	16	36½	41⅝	25¼	21¾	16¼	31
Average Mean Price of Ten Properties .	79¾	65⅝	71¼	90	108½	118⅛	110	95	75⅜

* $1.25 dividend and 20 per cent stock.

This table is compiled from official sources. At the foot of each column will be found the average yearly range of the ten stocks taken, and the average mean price of the same. These are exhibited for comparison in Chart IV.

The annexed diagram graphically represents the relations between the yearly average mean price of the ten stocks, named in the foregoing table, for each year from 1860 to 1885.

The period between 1860 and 1870 is marked with great events. A civil war, costing more than two billion dollars in money and thousands of lives, had been commenced and ended. The Atlantic Ocean had been spanned by an electric cable, and New York city had been placed in railway communication with San Francisco. In addition to these, the inflation of prices incident to a depressed currency, the presence of great speculative corners, the influence of stock dividends, in some cases doubling the capitalized stock of a railroad, makes it extremely difficult to form a correct opinion as to the true value of securities for that period. Indeed, it is but just to say that, when the foregoing table was being compiled, it was not expected that the results obtained would show any orderly arrangement whatever. The fact that such an arrangement is shown, is evidence that points to a conclusion which we cannot evade, namely, that the prices of stocks sold in the New York Stock Exchange exhibited a rise and fall, each extending over a period of years.

It may seem to some that the conclusion here reached

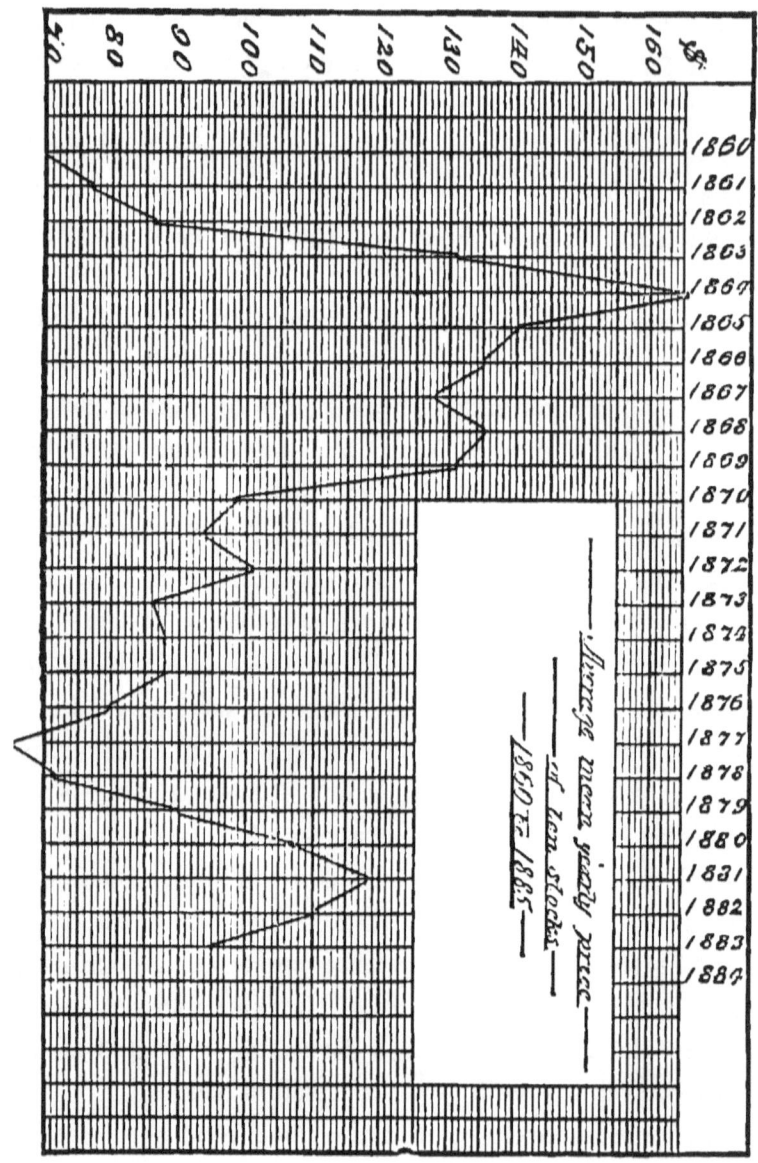

Average mean yearly price of ten stocks 1860 to 1885

bears no relation in value to the labor undergone in establishing it. To those we reply that ultimate truths are only found after long and patient search, and should be valued accordingly.

Taking into account the record of each year's history of the stock market, which we have recently passed over, we can readily see by referring to the diagram that the years 1864, 1872, and 1881 have been years when stocks, on an average, have reached high prices. The results, as brought together and exhibited in this diagram, would, if stated in words, fill volumes. They are instructive in that they show us that the laws with which we started out — the direction of motion and the rhythm of motion — are as operative here as elsewhere, and also points out the fact that in the future we may expect a repetition of high-priced years, after the present depression is passed.

In this review a few facts are worthy of notice. 1. Corners have almost disappeared, or have at least become relatively few. It has been noticed that these periods of excessive speculation carry with them their own corrective, and react with redoubled force upon the heads of their instigators, rather than upon the general community; and although prices or quotations may be temporarily affected by these gambling transactions, the inevitable laws of true value soon reassert themselves, and prices flow on in the natural channels.

2. Prices do not fall so low, neither do they rise so high, as in former years. The yearly range of the price of

stocks is decreasing, slowly it is true, but still the tendency to frequent and violent fluctuations is growing less. Prices are becoming more solidified, more fixed and definite.

3. The course of the prices of stocks is becoming more regular. Those early fluctuations which were made at the will of great operators now exhibit a well-defined course, which rises and falls with the course of general business outside the stock market.

During the growth of the stock exchange, from its comparatively few members with their simple methods, to its present state, composed of many brokers with methods of business comparatively complex, the history of the prices of stocks has undergone a change from the irregular to the comparatively regular, and from the indefinite to the comparatively definite, and so are justified those remarks with which this chapter commences. This tendency, as the years go by, will constantly grow more marked. Those securities which have only a speculative value must eventually succumb to those securities whose value is intrinsic, and among this latter class the price will fluctuate from year to year between decreasing limits. The time, however, before such events will be noticeably marked is so distant, and the decrease of the average yearly fluctuation is so small, that, though it may be an interesting study to notice these phenomena during our lifetime, the lessons which can be drawn from them are probably not practical. With the rhythms, however, which we have been considering, and whose highest points appear to be separated by intervals of from eight to nine years, it is otherwise. These phenomena will be treated in a subsequent chapter.

The following table shows the number and value of shares of stock sold at the New York Stock Exchange:—

NUMBER AND VALUE OF SHARES SOLD AT THE NEW YORK STOCK EXCHANGE (BONDS EXCLUDED).

Year.	Stocks, Shares.	Average Price.	Approximate Value.
1875	53,813,937	$53.20	$2,862,903,683
1876	39,926,990	53.40	2,132,050,483
1877	49,832,960	53.20	2,601,280,512
1878	39,875,593	54.10	2,157,269,581
1879	72,765,762	56.85	4,136,633,570
1880	97,919,099	69.60	6,819,086,054
1881	114,511,248	71.59	8,197,506,403
1882	116,307,271	66.12	7,689,453,436
1883	97,049,909	64.51	6,260,809,961
1884	96,154,971	61.77	5,939,500,000

The total sales of stocks are taken from the record kept by the *Journal of Commerce*. The values of sales are taken from the figures made up by *The Public*, except for 1884 and part of 1883, which are the figures of *The Commercial and Financial Chronicle*.

Bonds and unlisted securities are not included in this table, but these, as well as miscellaneous and bank stocks, rose and fell at about the same times as the average prices of the listed stocks.

CHAPTER VI.

EXCHANGE.

EXCHANGE may be divided into three classes : (1) primitive exchange, where goods were directly exchanged or bartered ; (2) mediæval exchange, where certain weights of iron, bronze, copper, or tin came to represent the value of goods ; and (3) modern exchange, which refers all mercantile values to one standard — gold. It is thought by some writers that even previous to bartering there was an interchange of goods by an exchange of presents, one party presenting certain goods with the expectation of receiving like favors from the presentee ; a custom of which traces still linger in the East. In Cairo, before entering into dealings with the merchant, you are invited to partake of coffee and cigarettes, and the dragoman will bring presents and expect presents while the negotiations are going on that end in the hire of his *dahabeah*. Presenting with the expectation of receiving like favors is, however, so much like bartering, that it may truly be called a distinction without a difference. It may safely be said that giving goods for goods is the oldest method of trading. Among a community of savage men, sufficiently advanced to carry on operations of hunting and fishing and tilling the ground, some will excel in making the implements by which these operations are carried on — bows, spears, baskets, nets, etc. The chances that each member equals each other member in the mechanical skill required, for instance, to make a spear, are as infinity to one; and so some one man's or family's make of spears come to be demanded because of their superiority of workmanship. There is a diversity of mechanical skill on the part of the spear-maker, and therefore a diversity of advantage for him in that direction. For the same reason others become to be known as makers of mats, as hunters, fishermen, warriors, and the like. But the warriors need bows and arrows, the hunters want spears, the fisherman wants woody fibre for making his baskets and nets, and all need either the fruits of the forest, or those nourishing roots or grains of which each family has a greater or less amount, and so an interchange of goods takes place between the members of that society. It is here to be noted that, though the goods are bartered, they are not exchanged promiscuously or hap-hazardly, but the value of each spear or bow or mat is measured by the labor that has been bestowed upon its production, and is exchangeable accordingly. One spear is exchangeable for four mats, and one bow for the carcass of a deer, and four fish represent the labor expended on a basket, etc.

Though at different times, and in different places, men have employed many standards of value, and accomplished the exchange in different ways, yet the basic principle of exchange which is here pointed out has never varied. You give so much of your services to me, and I will give so much of my services to you, is the underlying principle of all commercial transactions; and when the desires and abilities to fill these desires of the two parties are equalized, the exchange takes place. The buyer is satisfied. The seller is satisfied. Both parties are benefited. The buyer has received something he wanted, and given up that which he considered of less value, and exactly the same reason has influenced the seller to part with *his* goods, Homer speaks of this method of trading: "And thence, too, wine was got by the long-haired Achæans, some bartering it for bronze, and others the glistening steel; some hides, and some the cows themselves, and some again slaves."

At the present day, among all classes and races of people, this method of exchanging goods for goods (*i. e.* services for services) is going on, and in this country is known by the expressive though inelegant word, "swapping."

Keeping in view this principle of exchange of services for services, which we here see exemplified in all bartering transactions, we turn to the examination of those transactions which we have classed, for convenience, under the head of mediæval exchange, and we will discover that the principle remains the same, though the medium of exchange may differ in almost innumerable ways. Probably the metals came in to play a part in these tradings of goods, as being the things which all best liked to have, either for ornament or for use (and most probably the former, for the ornamental invariably precedes the useful), and so iron, copper, tin, bronze, being things that were not subject to decay, and being both ornamental and useful, to which add the fact that they represented a considerable amount of labor, came to have a greater relative value than bows, grain, wine, and hides. In early times these metals did service as a money, or a medium of exchange, and were of no particular shape, but interchangeable by weight. Later, certain weights were cast or shaped in the form of bars or spikes or rings, the latter being so contrived that it was possible for them to be hooked together and worn about the body. About the ninth century B. C., stamped coins appear, bearing an emblem of a sacred character, or of some legend relative to the formation of the state, which mark was a guarantee of their weight. The earliest Roman coin (about 578 B. C.) was a bronze oes, or as, — a brick-shaped mass weighing about a pound, and stamped with the representation of a sheep or an ox, and was probably interchangeable for them. The full pound of the as was gradually reduced, always retaining the twelve uncila subdivisions, till its full weight came to be no more than a quarter of an ounce. Silver was first coined in Rome about 281 B. C., and gold about 90 B. C. When we examine the history of the coins made of different metals, — bronze, copper, silver, gold, — and used as a medium of exchange by different people at different times, — the stater, the obolus, the drachma of the early Greeks; the shekel of the Jews; the oes, the uncia, the denarius, the sestertius, and the scrupulum of the Romans; the solidus, or gold nomisma of the Byzantine Empire; the silver skeatta, the copper styca of the Saxon kingdom of Northumbria; the quaint coins of the time of Alfred; the silver pennies, half pennies, groats, and the gold nobles of the reign of Edward III.; the silver florins of William IV., — we find that the principle of the exchange of these coins is the same as that upon which bartering is based; that is to say, an exchange of services for services. A certain weight of these metals, representing a certain amount of labor, is exchangeable for the same amount of labor, which may be either locked up in goods or in process of expenditure.

Other than metals, the wampum of the American Indian, the cowry shells of the East Indian, the salt brick of the Abyssinian, the kaniki,[1] sami-sami,[2] and sangomazzi,[3] of the interior African tribes, are considered good moneys, for the simple reason that they are a measure of services and are exchangeable for them.

Bullets were once a legal tender for debts under a shilling in Massachusetts; cakes of tea have passed as money in India, codfish in Iceland, beaver-skins in New Netherlands and Western America; iron was money in Sparta, lead in the Burman Empire, tin in old Britain, and platinum in Russia. In short, there is hardly any metal or any commodity which has not, at some time or other, served as a money. In looking over the whole field, we will observe

---

[1] Blue cloth.   [2] Red beads.   [3] Large marble-shaped beads.

one striking feature, namely, that as the iron, copper, or bronze, or cloth, or beads became plentiful, their purchasing power sank, and their places were supplied by something harder to get. We will observe how tin, copper, and steel were outranked by silver, platinum, and gold, and how eventually gold, as having locked up in it the largest amount of energy, outranked them all, and became the standard of commerce.

That, in modern exchange, gold is the standard of value, all admit, tacitly if not avowedly. When a new silver dollar is coined by the government, each citizen inadvertently asks, "What is it worth?" and the value of that piece of metal comes to be expressed in terms which refer to a gold standard. If money is a measure of labor or of service — and it has been so considered by all men in all times — then 23.22 grains of gold (the amount of gold in a dollar) must represent a certain amount of labor. That we may not deal with abstractions, let us represent the amount of intelligence, capital, and labor, which has been exerted to produce 23.22 grains of gold by the number 100. If by the expenditure of the force 100 there is produced $371\frac{1}{4}$ grains of silver (the amount of pure silver in the Bland or Buzzard dollar), the value of the two coins, the gold dollar and the silver dollar, may be said to be equal. The amount of energy, so to speak, locked up in $371\frac{1}{4}$ grains of silver, equals the amount of energy locked up in 23.22 grains of gold. Their exchanging power is therefore equal. If, however, to produce $371\frac{1}{4}$ grains of silver requires but the expenditure of the force 80, then it is manifest that they are not equal, and the price of silver falls. Or, again, the value of the silver and gold dollar being equal, if it require the expenditure of force, say 110, to produce 23.22 grains of gold, the price of gold may be said to rise. The exchanging power of silver, like any other commodity, is determined by the demand and supply, and as this varies from day to day and from hour to hour, the price consequently varies. Not having a stable value, then, unsuits it for use as a money among nations, and, indeed, many have discarded it, among others, England and Scandinavia. Legislators have endeavored to discover and fix the relation between the value of gold and silver time and again, and their efforts have been uniformly fruitless. The causes which govern the demand and supply of gold and silver are beyond the reach of legislative bodies, and any attempt to control them results in failure, — a failure paralleled by the attempt of Mrs. Partington to sweep up the Atlantic Ocean, or the endeavor of that pope who thought the comet would disappear upon his issuing a prohibitory bull. It is coming to be pretty generally understood that labor makes value and not law. It is true that the government has issued at times promises to pay money, that have, to a certain extent, answered all the purposes of money; but that these had an intrinsic value, no one has for a moment imagined. Their value does not reside in the green ink with which the back of the bill is covered, neither is it supposed that the style of the engraving, or the picture of Washington, or of the landing of Columbus, was the particular thing by virtue of which the bill circulated. The question was, Will the government pay me 23.22 grains of pure gold for each promise dollar that I hold? and, as confidence in the commercial integrity of the government increased or diminished, the bill came to have a greater or less value. When that faith became sight, the promise dollar became of the same value as the gold dollar. Had the fortunes of war, however, turned in the opposite direction, the greenback would undoubtedly have shared the present fate of its Confederate brother, and would have become, like the money of the colonial states, 'not worth a Continental.' There are at present the following kinds of legal tender in the United States : (1) gold coins ; (2) the silver dollar of $412\frac{1}{2}$ grains ; (3) United States notes (except for customs and interest on the public debt) ; (4) subsidiary silver coinage to the amount of five dollars; and (5) minor coins to the amount of twenty-five cents.

Modern commercial transactions are accomplished in three ways : (1) by barter or direct exchange of merchandise for merchandise ; (2) by those transactions classed as retail — the direct exchange of money for goods ; (3) by those transactions classed as book accounts, which are usually settled by a transfer of credits (*i. e.* beliefs that money will be paid). In that vast expanse of territory bounded in part by the oceans, the lakes, and the Gulf of Mexico, and inhabited by sixty millions of an active and energetic race, there are going on every day innumerable transactions in which money plays no part, except, possibly, as a mental measure of value. These dealings are known as bartering. What the amount, expressed in dollars, of these exchanges for a single day, or month, or year is, we have no means of knowing. That it represents, in the course of a year, a considerable sum, we may well believe. Similarly, of the amount of those transactions where money is directly exchanged for goods among the larger portion of its million traders who live and move and do business within the limits of that nation, there is no record. When we consider the different branches of business, — the clothing, drug, grocery, jewelry, hardware, drygoods, boot and shoe, and others that are carried on by business men in the forty or more large cities, in the thousands of towns and villages, and along the streets and country lanes by the hucksters and peddlers, we must admit that, could a record be kept of all these transactions where goods are directly exchanged for money, the total of a year's business would be a stupendous figure. Such data, valuable as they would be, can, however, never be collected.

There remains another class of transactions to be considered, namely, book accounts. One business man opens what is termed a book account with another man, if he has a belief that the buyer of his merchandise will pay. Such transactions are sometimes called "giving a line of credit," and the length of the line or amount of credit given is determined by the amount of faith which the seller has in the buyer. There are five ways by which book accounts may be liquidated : (1) by rendering a counter account; (2) by direct payment of money; (3) by giving a check; (4) by accepting a draft ; (5) by giving a promissory note. The first method, settlement by rendering a counter account, is quite common in the country districts. Thus A, a grocer, may owe B, a hardware dealer, $100; B buys his groceries of A, and when B's bill amounts to $100, each receipts his respective bill and they exchange accounts. Of the amount of this kind of trading going on among business men there is also no record. Accounts may be settled by direct payment of money. John Allen, a laborer, owes Messrs. Rose & Co., dealers in boots and shoes, $15. The account is settled and the books balanced when Mr. Allen pays $15 in gold, silver, or legal-tender notes. The amount of this kind of trading done in a year in the United States must be enormous. There is, however, no record of it. Checks — orders to pay money; drafts or bills of exchange — demands to pay money; and promissory notes — promises to pay money, — are used to pay debts, and of these we have a partial record, and so, indirectly, a record of the amount of business transactions carried on in the country for a day, month, or year. But before examining these, it is necessary that we should gain an idea of the proper functions of a bank, as it is from the inter-passage of such credit-rights between the banking institutions that we obtain a knowledge of their amount.

Banking, as we know it to-day, probably originated with

those London goldsmiths who received and kept in trust the moneys of the early English merchants, and paid it out upon their written orders. The convenience of this method of settling must have been apparent when contrasted with that earlier method of trading, where merchandise could only be acquired by the direct exchange of money for it. It is true that when new forms of credit, such as promissory notes, acceptances, and the like, arose with a more complex age, the transaction of a simple deposit of coin-money became a transaction in which coin-money plays but a little part, and credit-rights play a most important part. The central idea of a bank is, however, the same as formerly, — that it should receive the money and credits of its customers, and enter the amount of the same upon its books as a credit to the depositor. Furthermore, it must stand ready at any time to pay back in money the amount of its deposits when called for; but as the depositors never or rarely call for their money at the same time, and as most of the transactions between business men are settled by giving a check, in which case no money changes hands, but simply credits, the bank does not need to keep on hand in money the full amount of its deposits, and so loans a portion of its credit to whoever wants to buy it, provided always that the buyer will furnish good security. Besides loaning its deposits, a banking institution collects drafts, or bills of exchange, and discounts future paper of all kinds. From these three operations — loans, collections, and discounts, banks obtain the greater portion of their profits, and they may therefore be called institutions for the management of credits ; and a banker is known as a *dealer* in credits, buying some and selling others, much in the same manner as a hatter buys and sells hats. Among a number of banks it will unavoidably occur that, in the course of business, some banks will come to owe others and have other banks owing them ; and as the banks originally arose for the convenience of merchants in settling their debts, so the clearing-house has arisen for the convenience of banks in settling their differences. The New York Clearing-House is an association composed of about sixty-six banks, and its primary object of existence is to serve as a machine by means of which the debits and credits between those banks can be settled. Clearings or settlements are had each business day, each bank having credited to its account all the demand paper which it holds against the other banks, and being charged with all the demand paper which the other banks hold against it. The balances for or against a bank are usually payable in cash, and when this is done the clearing is completed.

We are now ready to go forward and determine just what the reports of the clearing-house include, and in what cases the settlements of book accounts do not appear. It is supposed that the reader has a sufficient acquaintance with the forms of checks, drafts, and promissory notes, and the manner in which they are used to settle accounts ; and therefore time and space need not be here used in presenting the forms and explaining the manner in which they are interchanged. But it must not be supposed that the returns of clearings of the New York banks represent the amount of checks, drafts, or notes that are circulating even among the citizens of the city of New York, much less among the people of the country. For instance, A and B each have an account with the First National Bank of New York, and during the course of business transactions A may give to B his check for $10,000, in which event A would be charged with that sum, and B would be credited with it upon the books of the First National when he made his daily deposit, and the check would *not* appear in the clearing-house. If, however, A gives his check to B, and B deposits it at the Park National Bank, the check *would* appear in the clearing-house as a demand from the Park National Bank upon the First National. What is here said concerning checks applies with equal force concerning drafts and promissory notes. Individual or firm acceptances, when made payable at banks, appear where parties to the transaction have deposit accounts at different banks, and do not appear where the parties to the transaction have deposit accounts at the same bank. Promissory notes, when due and made payable at banks, appear if parties to the transaction have deposit accounts at different banks. Promissory notes not made payable at banks do not appear, and, when made payable at the bank where both parties have deposit accounts, do not appear. These are a few of the cases of the transactions among the citizens of the city of New York, of which there is only a partial record, to which we must add all those other cases which occur in the settlements of the New York banks with their country correspondents, some of whose drafts pass through the clearing-house, and some do not. From this examination it would appear that the clearings, as representing the amount of business done, are, to a certain extent, illusive and misleading; yet, when we reflect that, in the average of cases, men will settle their debts in about the same manner, we cannot but believe that these data have *some* value. We must always bear in mind, however, that these returns of clearings are only a *reflection* of that vast amount of exchange here classed as bartering, retailing, and book accounts. Below is a table of the yearly clearings of the New York associated banks since 1875. These yearly clearings, it appears, increase and decrease along with the rise and fall of the price of iron, and the decrease and increase of the number of failures. They are exhibited for comparison in the chart on page 125. The clearings of the New York banks are about two thirds of the total clearings of the country: —

NEW YORK CLEARINGS.

1875 . . . . . $22,475,359,339	1880 . . . . . $38,614,448,223
1876 19,584,393,198	1881 49,376,882,883
1877 21,285,278,472	1882 46,916,955,031
1878 19,858,671,307	1883 37,434,300,872
1879 29,235,673,829	1884 30,985,871,165

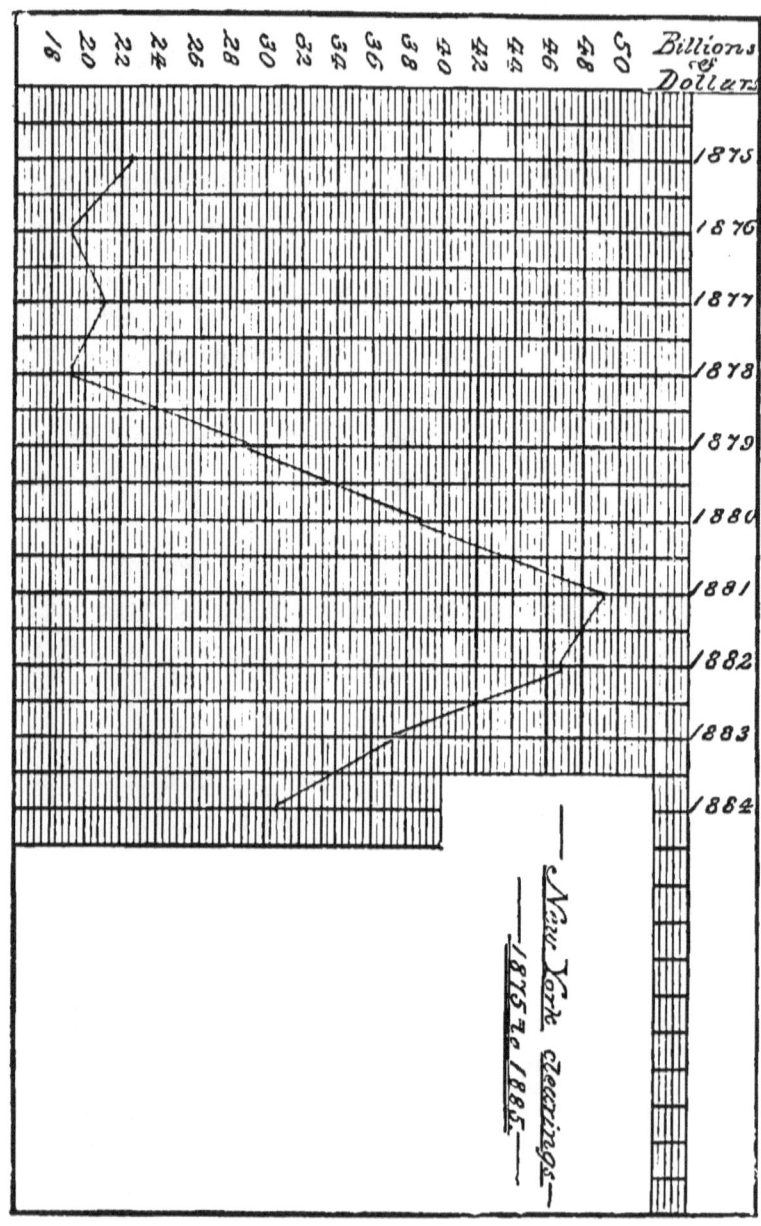

CHAPTER VII.

FOREIGN TRADE.

WHEN we make our morning toilet, we rarely think that the wool of which our garments are composed has, in all probability, been grown in Australia; that the soap we use has come from France or Italy; the tooth-brush from London, and the bristles from which it is made from the Russian Empire. Neither do we consider that the whiteness of the linen we wear can only be produced by the use of indigo brought from Central America. When we sit at our morning meal, the thought never enters our head that the oranges before us have come from the shores of the Mediterranean Sea, and that the coffee we drink and the sugar with which it is flavored can only be grown under the influence of a tropical sun. When, after breakfast, we draw on a rubber coat and go to our place of business through the storm, we do not think that the rubber with which the garment is thinly glazed was once the viscid juice of a tree which grows on the banks of some far-off Brazilian river. Yet all this and much more is the truth. Not only are the interests of all men of a country intertwined, but the same is true of all men whatsoever. The roast beef of England starts on its journey to the tables of the aristocracy from the great cattle-ranches of Western America. The wheat of the prairie States helps fight the battles of the Soudan. American cotton clothes the peasantry of the Old World, and the products of the Pennsylvania oil regions feed the lamps that hang in the temples of Jerusalem. Commerce sends her ships into every sea, and circles the globe with her rivers of trade. Consider the thousands of men engaged in transporting one article — the world's supply of tea; the hundreds of vessels which at this moment are sailing over the broad waste of the Pacific, engaged in this trade, braving, it may be, the dangers of the typhoon; add to these the ten thousand ships carrying the almost numberless products of the mine, the forest, and the plain, coming and going, crossing and recrossing, sailing through tropical calms, and furious, icy, northwestern gales, ever moving forward day and night, and all for what? — one purpose only — that your personal wants may be gratified. Looked at in this light, the figures of exports and imports, which to most minds are figures only, become alive with interest.

The trade which is carried on between countries is precisely mirrored by the trade which is carried on between individuals. The shoemaker exchanges his boots and shoes for clothing and bread; the carpenter his labor for money, and all other men are led to offer their services where they can receive the largest returns for them. Each man gives up that of which he wants less for that of which he wants more, and on the same principle all men of a country willingly exchange with other countries their surplus products for luxuries and articles which either are not made here or can be produced cheaper abroad. Articles of any description sent out of a country are called exports, and those brought to a country, imports. The value of a few of the leading articles exported from the United States in the year 1884 is given in the following table:—

Exports, 1884.	Value.	Exports, 1884.	Value.
Raw Cotton	$195,854,531	Lard	$25,305,953
Manufactured Cotton	11,535,941	Beef	15,257,364
Wheat	75,026,678	Pork	4,762,715
Corn	27,648,139	Mineral Oils (illuminating)	38,195,349
Flour	51,139,696		
Bacon and Hams	39,684,845	Tobacco (leaf)	17,765,760

The exports of this country consist mainly of the products of the extractive industries, cotton ranking first in value, followed by breadstuffs, animals and meats, mineral oils, wood, and tobacco. This fact, which can be verified by the foregoing table, is conclusive evidence that the manufacturing industries of the country are by no means as yet fully developed. The value of a few of the leading articles of import for the year 1883-4 is as follows:—

Imports, 1883-4.	Value.	Imports, 1883-4.	Value.
Brown Sugar	$91,154,315	Flax, Hemp, & Jute Stuffs	$22,769,091
Wool and Woollen Goods	50,718,646	Hides and Skins	22,350,906
Coffee	49,686,705	Fruits and Nuts	19,754,005
Silk and Manuf. of Silk	49,165,142	India Rubber and Gutta Percha	13,736,004
Various Manuf. of Cotton	29,917,785		
Tin and Tin Plate	23,612,691		

The tremendous growth of our foreign trade during the last twenty-five years is probably as much due to the progress of invention as to any other one cause. Modern mowers, reapers, and ploughs enable the American farmer of to-day to accomplish, in the same time, five times the amount of work of his father of fifty years ago. Railroads have been extended into fertile regions, which, but a few years before, were idle wilds, and, owing to the improvements made in rails, rolling-stock, and locomotives, rates have been cheapened so that it has been possible to lay down in Liverpool, at a profit, a portion of the vast crop of cereals of the Western States. Add to this the discovery of petroleum by Col. Drake; the improvements in the methods of killing and shipping beeves and hogs; the invention of the sewing machine by Howe; the practical application of electricity by Morse, Cyrus W. Field, and others; and lastly, the inventions of Bell and Edison, and we gain a faint idea of the tremendous influence exercised by the thousands of inventors whose work has been partly the cause, and partly the effect, of the improvement of manufactures and the extension of commerce.

The total value of domestic merchandise, coin, and bullion exported, and foreign merchandise, coin, and bullion re-exported in 1883-4, was $807,646,992. The total value of imports of merchandise, coin, and bullion in 1883-4 was $705,123,955. The sum of these total exports and imports would represent the total amount of business transactions carried on between this and other countries. To show the gross total amount of our foreign trade for each year, we have prepared the following table. The figures in the third column represent in dollars the sum of all our exports and imports of *every* kind and description, for each year, from July 1, 1861, to July 1, 1884:—

Years ending June 30.	Total Imports, Including merchandise, coin, and bullion.	Total Exports, Including foreign merchandise, coin, and bullion re-exported, and exports of domestic merchandise, coin, and bullion.	Grand Total, Exports and Imports.
1860	$362,166,254	$400,122,296	$762,288,550
1861	335,650,153	249,344,913	585,005,066
1862	205,771,729	227,558,141	433,329,870
1863	252,919,920	268,121,608	521,041,528
1864	329,562,895	264,284,529	593,847,424
1865	248,555,652	229,656,726	478,212,378
1866	445,512,158	434,903,593	880,415,751
1867	417,833,575	358,172,025	776,005,600
1868	371,624,808	375,737,001	747,361,809
1869	437,314,255	343,256,077	780,570,332
1870	462,377,587	450,927,434	913,305,021
1871	541,493,708	541,262,166	1,082,755,874
1872	640,338,766	524,055,120	1,164,393,886
1873	663,617,147	607,087,891	1,270,705,038
1874	595,861,248	642,913,445	1,238,774,693
1875	553,906,153	605,573,853	1,159,480,006
1876	476,677,871	596,890,973	1,073,568,844
1877	492,097,540	658,637,457	1,150,734,997
1878	466,872,846	728,594,091	1,195,466,937
1879	466,085,141	735,425,384	1,201,510,525
1880	760,919,875	852,936,843	1,613,856,718
1881	753,240,125	921,784,193	1,675,024,318
1882	767,111,964	799,959,736	1,567,071,700
1883	751,670,305	855,659,735	1,607,330,040
1884	705,123,955	807,646,992	1,512,770,947

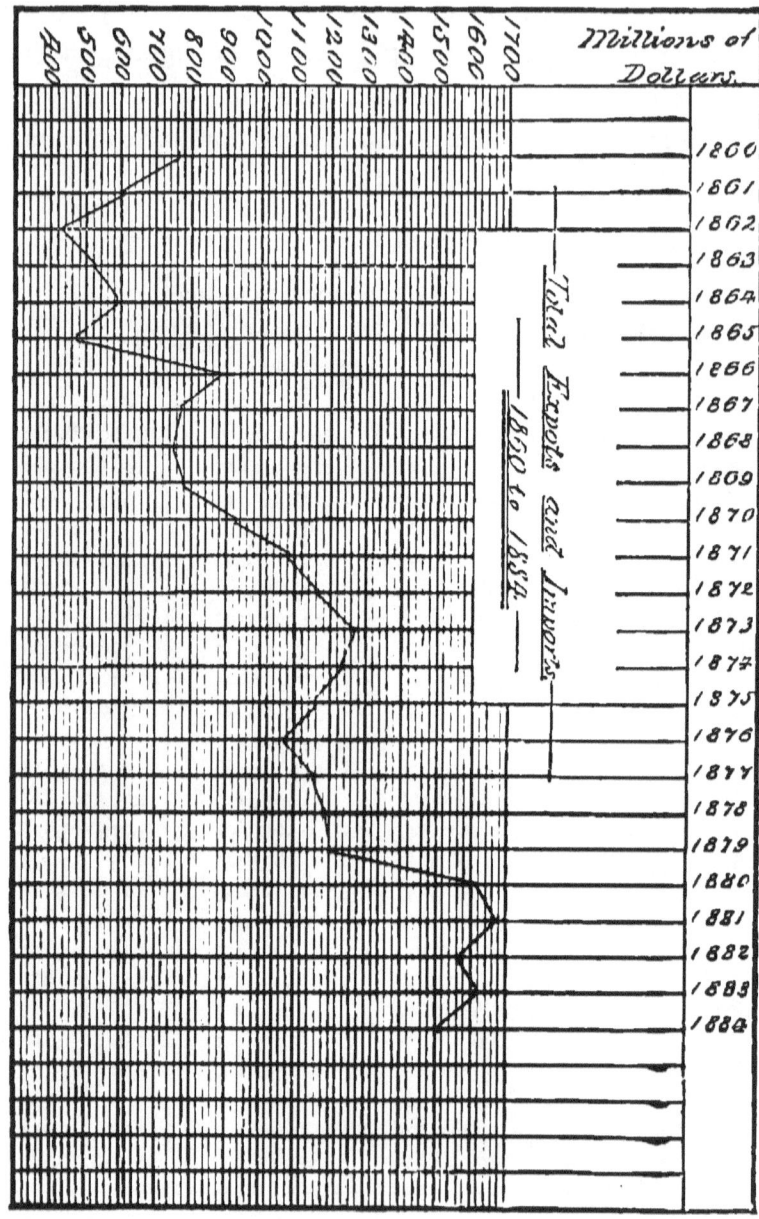

While the growth of business relations between the United States and foreign countries has doubled in the last twenty years, that growth has by no means been regular and uniform, but consists of wave-like movements, corresponding in character and agreeing in time with those movements which we have noticed when examining the record of failures, price of iron, etc., as the annexed chart shows. Previous to 1865-6 the figures are not reliable, as only the exports and imports of the Northern States are included.

While considering this subject, it is interesting to note what proportion our foreign trade bears to our domestic trade. To show this relation, the following table has been prepared:—

Total clearings of country, 1883	$51,570,200,000
Total foreign trade, 1883-1884	1,512,770,947
Percentage of domestic trade to total trade (about)	97 per cent
Percentage of foreign trade to total trade (about)	3 per cent

The percentage of foreign trade to total trade must, however, be considerably lower than this (probably not over one per cent), as the clearings do not faithfully represent the total amount of business done in the country, as has been before pointed out.

CHAPTER VIII.

GRAIN.

THERE seems to be an impression among business men, that, to increase our crops, we only need plant a larger acreage, and, presto, we obtain a larger yield. This is a view which, plausible enough at first sight, will not stand the test of investigation. Let us examine some of the conditions under which our crops are grown and harvested.

"Climate influences (Census Report, 1880) are the controlling conditions of grain-growing the world over, and grain countries and grain regions are made so by the climate and not by the soil. The difference between a desert and a fertile region is often one simply of rainfall, and while rain is an absolute necessity, so also is a certain climate as regards temperature."

Considered according to the rainfall of spring and summer, or the six growing months, 97.2 per cent of the total crop of cereals is produced where it is between 15 and 30 inches; considered according to mean annual temperature, 91.4 per cent of the total crop of cereals is produced where it is between 40 and 60 degrees, and 70 per cent where the mean temperature of January (average midwinter temperature) is below 30 degrees.

Another fact worthy of notice is that 52.9 per cent of

the cereal crop is grown in regions where the elevation above the sea is from 500 to 1,000 feet, and 91.7 per cent is produced where the elevation is between 100 and 1,500 feet.

The general character of the soil upon which the crop of cereals is grown, is known as drift, which, as geologists tell us, was formed by the accumulated debris of glaciers and icebergs in a remote period of the earth's history,— the method of formation corresponding in a certain degree to the processes which formed, and are now forming, the banks of Newfoundland. The so-called drift soils occupy the principal territory lying north of the Ohio and east of the Missouri rivers, and in five of the principal States occupying that region, namely, Ohio, Indiana, Illinois, Missouri, and Iowa, 52.7 of the total crop of cereals is grown.

Now, while it is possible for us to control the height above the sea at which we sow our grain, and to select the best soil upon which to plant it, yet we can never control the climatic conditions which make or break the crop. This work is done by the sun, and not by the farmer. As proof of this assertion, let us compare two years of the production and acreage of the corn crop, the principal cereal of the country, as follows : —

CORN.

Year.	Average Acreage.	Crop.
1880	62,317,842	1,717,434,543
1883	68,301,889	1,551,066,895
	5,984,047	166,367,648

In 1883 there were sown 5,984,047 acres more than in 1880, and the crop was 166,367,648 bushels less than that of 1880.

Other comparisons could readily be made of wheat, oats, or other crops, but this is sufficient to show us that it is not always that we can increase the crop by increasing the acreage.

Another fallacy which appears to be firmly rooted in the minds of most business men is that large crops necessarily make good business. Let us examine. By reference to the record of failures we shall find that the years 1874, 1875, 1876, and 1877 were poor business years, and 1879, 1880, 1881, and 1882 were good business years. During the former period each acre sown produced 25.3 bushels of corn per year, and each bushel brought 42.9 cents. During the latter period each acre produced 24.7 bushels of corn per year, and each bushel brought 46.1 cents. The crop during these latter four years was smaller to the acre than during the four years of depression, and brought a larger price. Manifestly, then, the cause of commercial depression cannot be laid to the partial failure of the corn crop, for during the period of the last commercial depression the crop was larger per acre than when the boom was in motion.

In endeavoring to reconcile with the facts the opinion that large crops make good business, we have unwittingly come in sight of another truth, which it will be well to note; namely, that the farmer receives more money for a small crop than he does for a large one. Thus the crop of corn in 1880 was exceptionally large, being 1,717,434,543 bushels, valued at $679,714,499, while the crop of 1881 was 1,194,916,000 bushels, valued at $759,482,170. The crop of 1881 was, in round numbers, 525,000,000 bushels less than that of 1880, and brought $80,000,000 more money. This, it may be remarked, while it was a good thing for the farmers that had the corn, was a poor thing for those who had to buy it. If we examine the statistics of the wheat, oats, rye, or barley crops, we shall find that, as a rule, they present the same facts, from which can be drawn the same conclusions, viz: that the acreage does not make the crop; that the farmer receives more money for a small crop than he does for a large one, and that the crop raised in years of poor business is larger, per acre, than the crop raised in good business years. The wheat crop is an exception in the latter respects, the yield averaging 12 bushels per acre in poor business years, and 12 1-2 bushels per acre in good business years.

Taking everything into consideration, the alternation between heavy and light harvests, which do really occur, and the alternation between high and low prices when these crops are sold, does not account for those fluctuations between good and bad times which we see in the commercial world. This cause is not sufficient to produce the results, and while undoubtedly good crops are a factor among the causes which make up a business boom, it is not necessarily the only factor, and a careful study of the tables given, will convince the mind that it is really a very small factor. These points it may be well to repeat.

First. The number of acres planted is no criterion of the crop.

Second. Large yields per acre do not necessarily make good business.

Third. In the aggregate, farmers receive more money for a small crop than they do for a large one.

Fourth. The crop of cereals is dependent more on climatic conditions than any other phenomena.

Upon what do climatic conditions depend? As far as we know, at present there is but one answer, — the sun. Those changes, then, in the average yield per acre of the corn crop, which we observe from year to year, are, at the ultimate analysis, traceable to like changes going on in the sun. What are those changes going on in the sun, and do they present any regular order? We answer that some of the phenomena which the sun presents have been accurately observed and found to be rhythmic, namely: the number of spots upon the sun's surface have been found to undergo an increase and decrease ranging over a period of about eleven years. (These sun spots will have almost disappeared in 1888 and will probably be numerous in 1894.) These, it has been observed, undoubtedly influence the variations of the magnetic needle, but whether they have any influence over the production, and therefore the price, of cereals, is still a debatable question. Until that question is settled it will be impossible to reduce the growing of grain to a science, that is, to know what years to expect large, and what years to expect small harvests, and to plant accordingly.

There is considerable testimony upon both sides of the question as to whether the sun spots influence the weather. For instance, Mr. Stone, at the Cape of Good Hope, and Dr. Gould. in South America, consider that the observations taken at those places show a slight diminution of the earth's temperature—amounting to one or two degrees—at the period of sun-spot maximum. Mr. Chambers concludes, from twenty-eight years' observations, that the hottest are those of most sun spots. These two, it would seem, contradict each other. Glenick concludes that all are wrong together, and that there really is no change whatever; while Professor Langley, of the Allegany Observatory, concludes that, though the sun spot itself is cooler than the rest of the surface, after a good deal of experiment and observation, he is prepared to say that there is no direct evidence that the sun is hotter at one time than another.

Thus the case stands. Years ago, the ignorant thought the sun had no influence whatever upon cereal or any other kind of life; to-day the inquiring disagree as to the character of that influence, and in the future, after the phenomena there exhibited are carefully studied and compared with the phenomena exhibited here, the wise will agree that changes (it may be other than changes in sun-spot frequency) are really going on in the sun, and are the direct causes of the variations which the crop reports present. Agriculture cannot be reduced to a science until it can be known with reasonable accuracy what kind of seasons we will have ; and we can tell what the character of the seasons will be only by long years of observation of the causes which produce their variableness. That these causes, when found, will present a rhythm there can be no doubt. This, as we have before learned, is the method of movement among all natural phenomena, and, by extending these rhythms into the future, we may form approximate judgments of the character of coming seasons, and, like Joseph, be able to predict the coming years of famine and of plenty, and so make life happier and easier to hundreds of millions of toilers upon the earth's surface.

One effect that such knowledge would cause, would be that prices of cereals would not rise so high, neither would they fall so low, as at present, but would fluctuate with but minor rhythms upon each side of an established mean. The large crop of grain produced in a season of plenty would not be sold at the low prices which always accompany large crops, but be held in granaries to be distributed when crops became small and prices high. These remarks, however, based upon a supposition, must be taken for what they are worth, and have nothing to do with the general tenor of this work.

The evidence contained in this chapter is, we think, sufficiently conclusive that the crops are mainly the work of the sun, and influence in but a small degree the business rhythms which we have been considering in former chapters. We append tables of yearly production, acreage, value, etc., of corn, wheat, oats, rye, and barley, for comparison.

These tables are furnished by the **Department of Agriculture at Washington.**

CORN.

Years.	Total Production	Total Area of Crop.	Total Value of Crop.	Average Value per Bushel.
	Bushels.	Acres.	Dollars.	Cents.
1871	991,898,000	34,091,137	478,275,900	48.2
1872	1,092,719,000	35,526,836	435,149,290	39.8
1873	932,274,000	39,197,148	447,183,020	48.0
1874	850,148,500	41,036,918	550,043,080	64.7
1875	1,321,069,000	44,841,371	555,445,930	42.0
1876	1,283,827,500	49,033,364	475,491,210	37.0
1877	1,342,558,000	50,369,113	480,643,400	35.8
1878	1,388,218,750	51,585,000	441,153,405	31.8
1879	1,547,901,790	53,085,450	580,486,217	37.5
1880	1,717,434,543	62,317,842	679,714,499	39.6
1881	1,194,916,000	64,262,025	759,482,170	63.6
1882	1,617,025,100	65,659,546	783,867,175	48.5
1883	1,551,066,895	68,301,889	658,051,485	42.4
Total	16,831,057,078	659,307,639	7,324,986,781	
Annual average	129,469,698	50,715,972	563,460,532	43.5

WHEAT.

Years.	Total Production.	Total Area of Crop.	Total Value of Crop.	Average Value per Bushel.
	Bushels.	Acres.	Dollars.	Cents.
1871	230,722,400	19,943,893	290,411,820	125.8
1872	249,997,100	20,858,359	310,180,375	124.0
1873	281,254,700	22,171,676	323,594,805	115.0
1874	309,102,700	24,967,027	291,107,895	94.1
1875	292,136,000	26,381,512	294,580,990	100.0
1876	289,356,500	27,627,021	300,259,300	103.7
1877	364,194,146	26,277,546	394,695,779	108.2
1878	420,122,400	32,108,560	326,346,424	77.7
1879	448,756,630	32,545,950	497,030,142	110.8
1880	498,549,868	37,986,717	474,201,850	95.1
1881	380,280,090	37,709,020	453,790,427	119.0
1882	504,185,470	37,067,194	444,602,125	88.2
1883	421,086,160	36,455,593	383,649,272	91.1
Total . . .	4,689,744,164	382,100,068	4,784,451,204	
Annual average	360,749,551	29,392,313	368,034,708	102.0

OATS.

Years.	Total Production.	Total Area of Crop.	Total Value of Crop.	Average Value per Bushel.
	Bushels.	Acres.	Dollars.	Cents.
1871	255,743,000	8,365,809	102,570,030	40.1
1872	271,747,000	9,000,769	91,315,710	33.6
1873	270,340,000	9,751,700	101,175,750	37.4
1874	240,369,000	10,897,412	125,047,530	52.0
1875	354,317,500	11,915,075	129,499,930	36.5
1876	320,884,000	13,358,908	112,865,900	35.1
1877	406,394,000	12,826,148	118,661,550	29.2
1878	413,578,560	13,176,500	101,945,830	24.6
1879	363,761,320	12,683,500	120,533,294	33.1
1880	417,885,380	16,187,977	150,243,565	36.0
1881	416,481,000	16,831,600	193,198,970	46.4
1882	488,250,610	18,494,691	182,978,022	37.5
1883	571,302,400	20,324,962	187,040,264	32.7
Total	4,791,053,770	173,815,051	1,717,076,345	
Annual average	368,542,598	13,370,389	132,082,796	35.8

RYE.

Years.	Total Production.	Total Area of Crop.	Total Value of Crop.	Average Value per Bushel.
	Bushels.	Acres.	Dollars.	Cents.
1871	15,365,500	1,069,531	12,145,646	79.0
1872	14,888,600	1,048,654	11,363,693	76.3
1873	15,142,000	1,150,355	11,548,126	76.2
1874	14,990,900	1,116,716	12,870,411	85.8
1875	17,722,100	1,359,788	13,631,900	76.9
1876	20,374,800	1,468,374	13,635,826	66.9
1877	21,170,100	1,412,902	12,542,895	59.2
1878	25,842,790	1,622,700	13,592,826	52.6
1879	23,639,460	1,625,450	15,507,431	65.6
1880	24,540,829	1,767,619	18,564,560	75.6
1881	20,704,950	1,789,100	19,327,415	93.3
1882	29,960,037	2,227,889	18,439,194	61.5
1883	28,058,583	2,214,754	16,300,503	58.1
Total	272,400,649	19,873,832	189,470,426	
Annual average	20,953,896	1,528,756	14,574,648	69.6

BARLEY.

Years.	Total Production.	Total Area of Crop.	Total Value of Crop.	Average Value per Bushel.
	Bushels.	Acres.	Dollars.	Cents.
1871	26,718,500	1,177,666	21,541,777	80.6
1872	26,846,400	1,397,082	19,837,733	73.9
1873	32,044,491	1,387,106	29,333,529	91.5
1874	32,552,500	1,580,626	29,983,769	92.1
1875	36,908,600	1,789,902	29,952,082	81.3
1876	38,710,500	1,766,511	25,735,110	66.5
1877	34,441,400	1,614,654	22,028,044	64.0
1878	42,245,630	1,790,400	24,483,315	58.0
1879	40,283,100	1,680,700	23,714,444	58.9
1880	45,165,346	1,843,329	30,090,742	66.6
1881	41,161,330	1,967,510	33,862,513	82.3
1882	48,953,926	2,272,103	30,768,015	62.9
1883	50,136,097	2,379,009	29,420,423	58.7
Total . . .	496,167,820	22,646,598	350,751,496	
Annual average	38,166,755	1,742,046	26,980,884	70.7

CHAPTER IX.

THE BALANCING OF PRICES, OR EQUILIBRATION.

IN all commercial transactions, price is the resultant of four elements: a desire and an ability to purchase a commodity on the part of the buyer, and a desire and an ability to deliver a commodity on the part of the seller; and by the word commodity we mean, in this case, not alone wheat, corn, iron, and potatoes, but also all labor, whether manual or professional, and all things whatsoever that are exchanged or are capable of exchange. Not only have the hod-carrier, the carpenter, and the mason, their price at which they value their labor, but also the salary of the lawyer, the doctor, the clergyman, rises and falls as the demand, and ability to pay for their services, on the part of others, increases or diminishes. A change in either the desire or ability of a buyer to purchase, or a change in either the desire or ability to deliver on the part of the seller, causes a change in price. One illustration will suffice. The present price of corn is sixty cents a bushel. Why should it be that price and no other? Our answer is that there are a certain set of men who have the desire to buy and the ability to pay for corn, which means and desire they place at sixty cents for each bushel, and opposite to them are another set of men who, having the corn, are willing to take sixty cents per bushel for the labor of producing it and bringing it to market. Hence the exchange is effected. If from any cause, however, the supply of corn is diminished, then arises, among those who wish to purchase, a rivalry as to who shall have the corn, and the sellers are offered more than sixty cents for their labors in producing and ability to deliver the commodity, and the price rises. On the other hand, if, from any cause, the supply of corn is more than is the desire and ability of the buyers to purchase, the price falls.

This law of supply and demand has been so well stated by writers on Political Economy, that, without further attempts to justify it, we will take it for granted. Briefly stated it is as follows: The price of a commodity rises when the demand is greater than the supply. The price of a commodity falls when the supply is greater than the demand. Those high prices which, from time to time, occur in the iron, stock, and wages market, must be the periods when the total desire of the community for iron, stocks, and labor, is increasing faster than is the ability to supply that desire. Those times when the price of iron, stocks, or wages reaches the lowest point must be the periods when the ability to supply iron, stocks, or labor is greater than is the demand for them. The ideal price of a commodity, then, is the mean between the two extremes, supply and demand, — a time when interchange is well regulated and evenly balanced, keeping the consumer and

THE BALANCING OF PRICES. 147

producer steadily and evenly at work ; a time when there is neither great over-production of any commodity, nor is there great under-production ; and when the price of all things will fluctuate between relatively narrow limits. Will that time ever arrive? A few illustrations will here serve our purpose.

Children, when swinging under the forest trees, sometimes, after having gotten a 'good start,' sit quietly on the swing-board and let the vibrations to and fro grow smaller and smaller till they become invisible. If we ask the cause of these slowly decreasing motions, we shall find that the force originally imparted by the lad who swung the child has continually undergone subtractions by the force which the resistance of the air presents, and hence the equilibrium is reached when all the original force has been counteracted. Note further examples. A stone, when thrown into the water, produces ripples that, however inconsiderable in size near by, gradually widen and disappear in insensible fluctuations. The musical vibrations which are produced by a band are soon dispersed in the atmosphere in ever-decreasing undulations, and are radiated into space. Similarly the heat from a cinder or from a large molten mass of iron is, in time, transferred to the air, and its temperature becomes the same as that of surrounding bodies. The swinging pendulum, no matter how long the arm or how heavy the weight, at last becomes quiet. Even the heavenly bodies must suffer some retardation by the resistance of the ether through which they pass, and it is believed, though it has not been measured, that the daily rotation of the earth is growing slower, owing to the friction caused by the trade winds and the tidal wave. "Inequalities in the lunar motions, not accounted for by the theory of gravitation," says Professor Newcomb, "really exist, and in such a way that the mean motion of the moon between 1800 and 1875 was really less (i. e. slower) than between 1720 and 1800." Among phenomena this seems to be the rule: Any single and constant force becomes in time divided into lesser forces, and these lesser forces tend to equalize each other. If in summer we place a small plate of iron under the direct influence of the sun's rays, we will observe that the outer particles become first heated, and these, by a process of rhythmical movements, give up part of their motion to their fellows, and eventually the whole mass becomes of the same temperature; that is, each particle has equal motion.

From observations of the method of action of a vast number of phenomena, including those successively changed forms which have arisen during the evolution of the Solar System, down to those which are continually going on in the rearrangements of societies and of individual life, and which manifestly cannot here be treated in detail, men have been led to conclude that not only is all motion in the line of least resistance, and rhythmic, but in the rhythms which each phenomenon presents is a tendency to equilibrium. Commercial affairs are no exception. In England a few centuries ago the difference in the price of grain that occurred between harvests was greater than now occurs in twenty years. Farmers sowing a large quantity of wheat would find themselves overburdened with, to them, useless bread, and the price would sink to nothing. The next year they would plant but very little or none at all, and hence a famine would be caused and the price would rise to fabulous amounts. There is no fact more easily capable of proof than this, that as a community becomes larger and more complex, the prices of its commodities become more stable and firm. If the value of a service or of a commodity is a relation between the desires of men, and if, as we have reason to believe, the relations between men continually tend to grow into a greater harmony of desires· ·a belief that in our day is expressed by the familiar though ambiguous phrase, 'The greatest good to the greatest number,' — then it must necessarily follow that the price of all articles will eventually fluctuate between lesser and lesser limits, in a proportion co-incident to the gradually increasing intertwined interests which each society displays. However, the evidences that prices really tend to equilibrium are sufficient without the above illustration.

We know that the power originally exercised by a king or a despot has, except among a few uncivilized nations, disappeared, and the will of a majority has been put in its place. The tendency of advancing civilization is to more and more place power in the hands of the many, and substract it from the hands of the few, and that tendency, carried to its fullest extent, means that the government of all and by all shall eventually take the place of the government of one or of a few. Formerly it was thought that men were made for governments; now it is thought that governments are made for men. We know that wars are gradually decreasing in frequency, that the tendency among civilized nations is to cease cutting each other's throats, and to seek rather the conquests of peace than the conquests of arms. Formerly that country that won the greatest battles was considered the most advanced—now the country that does the most business is considered the most civilized. With the decrease of militarism, and the increase of the power of the citizen as against the power of the State, has gone an increase in business relations. And we know that, in these business relations, competition is constantly increasing. That which at first contributes to but one man or set of men, is, during the course of events, divided among many, and so works to the best good of all. As soon as it is discovered that a railroad corporation is earning large dividends on its stock, another one is built, and the business before done by one is divided between the two.[1] The second road requires as many engines, cars, and bridges as the first, and also needs as many men to run it. This increase of workers generates, in the towns through which the railroad passes, an increase in the number of retail

---

[1] The New York & West Shore is a case in point.

stores. There must necessarily be more goods consumed, and consequently a larger demand for dealers in dry goods, groceries, drugs, jewelry, etc.

So, too, with the men who build cars, bridges, and locomotives. Increased demand means increased profits ; increased profits mean increase of competition ; and increased competition means final equilibration.

Among all other dealers the tendency is the same. The wholesale dealer in dry doods finds that his business is continually being cut into by other and new concerns. The retail dealer in drugs starts a store wherever he thinks it will pay, no matter if there are several other stores in the town ; and, in a free-license town, the surprising fertility of saloons shows how, even in this business, the tendency of all trade is to divide among many that which was before enjoyed only by a few. And thus is constantly going on a quiet yet certain destruction of monopoly, and a betterment of the condition of all.

But it may be objected, while all this is very true concerning trades, it is certainly not true concerning manufactures. Witness, for instance, in the cooper's trade, the number of hands employed in 1880 had increased eleven per cent in ten years, while the number of establishments had decreased twenty-two per cent in the same time ; this showing a concentration of capital as well as of labor, and, if this continue to be the case, the rich are growing richer and the poor poorer. Let us examine. If we take the trouble to look into the matter, we shall find that making of coopers' products has, within the last ten years, become relatively complex. One man formerly began and finished a pail, even to making and putting on the bail. Now the case is different. Each operation in pail-making is done by a different set of workmen, and the result is that we now have better pails and cheaper than ever before possible. Steam and water power have to a great extent taken the place of hand power, and the result has been beneficial to all, because the commodities furnished are better in quality and cheaper in price than formerly. There is a limit, however, which concentration of labor and capital cannot pass. When the manufacture of an article becomes perfected; when the best possible machines and workmen produce the best possible products, — then if an increased demand springs up, there is no plan to follow but to enlarge old factories or build new ones; and, when this is done, workers are increased, profits are divided, and equilibrium is more closely attained.

A most important fact in this connection is that the laborer is receiving a constant increase in wages from period to period. Thus the average yearly income of all employees of all classes engaged in manufacturing was, in 1880, $347; in 1870, $314;[1] in 1860, $289; and in 1850, $247. While the income of the laborer is rising, the cost of the necessaries of life is decreasing. Boots and shoes, clothing and food products, with the possible exception of

---

[1] In currency, $377. The average price of gold for 1869 was $1.35; for 1870 was $1.15. We have taken $1.20 as the average price.

meats, were never before so cheap as at the present day. This tendency to improvement in the material affairs of the laborer, while it is slow, like all other processes of development in nature, is still in the right direction, and would seem to indicate a time when, among all people, there will be a better balance of moneyed wealth.

The returns of agricultural statistics acquaint us with facts of equal importance. The number of farms was returned in 1860 as about 2,000,000; in 1870, as about 2,500,000, and in 1880, at about 4,000,000. The average size of farms for each of these periods was respectively 199, 153, and 134 acres. In 1880, 74 per cent of the farms were worked by their owners, 8 per cent were rented for a fixed money rental, and 18 per cent were worked for a share of the product. Not only do the great majority of the farmers own their lands, but from year to year there seems to be going on a gradual division and splitting up of larger farms into fragments, and these smaller farms become the property of the many. This tendency, carried to its finality, means complete and universal division of land among all members of a society, and is a striking illustration of that universal equilibrium towards which we are inevitably progressing.

When we consider the enormous grants of land made by our legislators to private corporations, and when we consider all the direct and indirect means which are employed by the selfish and the unscrupulous for personal aggrandizement, and which has lately shown one of its phases in the matter of the Oklahoma "boomers;" the fact that land is being divided and redivided among the people of the country until at last all, or a great majority, shall hold small lots of land is, to say the least, surprising and suggestive.

And this is being accomplished not by any far-sighted legislation; not through the influence of an enlightened public opinion, but seems rather to be the method by which nature works for the eventual good and welfare of the race. Nor can this peculiarity be explained away as the result of increase of population, for the increase in the number of farms from decade to decade was far ahead of the percentage of increase in the population of the country districts for the same time.

Not only is land being divided and wages are increasing, but a social equilibrium is also progressing. It is a noticeable fact that the most advanced, as a class, have fewer offspring, and fail usually to transmit to them the powers by which they have raised themselves above mediocrity, while the children of the farmer and of the frontiersman are numerous, active, and energetic, and from this class spring the men who are to lead their fellows in the future, to be again replaced by new families successively arising. Thus there is going on a circulation from lower to higher, and from higher to lower, which cannot but eventually end in the good of all.

Still further evidence pointing in this direction can be observed when we inquire as to the profits which capital

THE BALANCING OF PRICES. 155

earns, and we find that such profits are undergoing a constant diminution. From an examination of the books of two cotton mills in New England, where the capital and number of laborers had remained the same, it was discovered that the price of the goods had decreased 22 per cent in 44 years, the amount of profit per yard required to pay ten per cent on the capital used had decreased from 1.18 cents to 0.43 cents, while the wages of the operatives per hour had increased 96 per cent in the same time. The diminishing proportion of the price which goes to capital well illustrates the tendency of profits to fall with the increase of capital. A comparison of railroad rates will show us the same truth; thus the charge per ton per mile in 1855 was 3.27 cents as compared with 0.89 cents in 1883. The number of tons of freight moved one mile in 1883 by railroads of New York State was 9,286,216,628; at the rate of 1855 would cost $303,659,283; actual cost, 1883, $83,464,919: saving to people and apparent loss to capital, $220,194,364. With the increase of railroads made possible by increasing business and by the paralleling of roads now bonded and stocked for four or five times their actual cost price, and by the further improvements and inventions which are being added day by day to existing lines, the present railroad rates must undergo still further reduction, and the minimum rate will be reached only when complete industrial equilibration is established; that is to say, when capital becomes equally or approximately balanced between all citizens. That the rate of interest, that is, the amount of money paid for the use of capital, is constantly growing less, is a marked characteristic of our time. The experience of our own government in placing loans for the past one hundred and fifty years abounds with illustrations of this tendency. Early colonial loans bore a rate of interest, the market price of securities in gold being considered, varying from twelve to fifty per cent per annum in the currency of that day. With the cessation of war, and the consequent growth of industrial pursuits, has gone a reduction of interest rates, and at the present day it is thought by some prominent financiers that a government bond bearing two per cent interest, interest and principal payable in gold, would quickly secure a loan of almost any amount, if made for legitimate purposes. Advance in this direction has not as yet ceased, nor can it be expected that it will cease before that ideal state is reached when the use of capital will be free.

While to some it may be difficult to see, in the affairs of every day life, just how this is being accomplished, that difficulty will be to a certain extent overcome when we take an intelligent view of the story of progress. He who reads history aright will see in it more than the story of the lives of kings and the intrigues of courts. To him, the sound of the drums, the blare of the trumpets, the waving plumes, the flaunting banners, the on-rush of the assailants, will have but a passing significance. He will find in its pages the death of monarchy and the broadened life of the individual: the decay of feudalism, tyranny, and slavery, and the elevation of the masses to citizenship. He will note, for instance, the remarkable change that has gone on in the theatre since the time of Marlowe, whose plays abound in murders, assassinations, and lewdness, as contrasted with the mirth-provoking comedies and airy operettas of the present day. He will observe that the tastes of the people no longer require that the heads of criminals should adorn London Bridge, and that murmurs no longer arise among the populace because the suffering victim is not disembowelled and burnt before their eyes. He will see that learning is no longer the monopoly of the monasteries, and that free speech, free religion, free government are no longer decried; in other words, he will see that equilibrium is slowly being attained; and from that study, so conducted, he will be led to believe that where equal laws affect the units of a community alike, each citizen of that community will become, in course of time, equal in property, wealth, learning, political power, and social condition with each other citizen. Whether this be a true statement or not, we at least know that, as compared with the civilization of one or two hundred years ago, there is a vastly better balance of property, wealth, and civil freedom between all people than ever before in the history of the globe, and upon this point there can be no doubt.

The inference that, as advance in this direction has hitherto been the rule, it will henceforth be the rule, may be considered a plausible speculation. When it is shown that this peculiarity is a result of a universal law, and that in virtue of that law it must continue, then it becomes reasonably certain that equilibrium will, at some far distant time, be reached. These considerations, however, have for us only an indirect importance, and their treatment belongs properly to the department of social science, and need not here receive full exposition.

Probably as good an illustration of the progress of the equilibration of prices as any that can be pointed out among industrial enterprises is that contained in the history of the oil trade. Fluctuating in its early history, often in a single year, from twenty cents to twenty dollars per barrel, the highest and lowest points have gradually approached each other, until at the present day they are comparatively balanced, or at least, the price fluctuates between relatively narrow limits. It is here to be noticed that exactly the same cause — (competition) which has accomplished this result in the oil trade is at work in every other industry and will eventually bring forth the same results.

That tendency to diminish in the average of liabilities which is observable in the table of failures, and that tendency to fluctuate between lesser limits which can be seen in the constantly diminishing numbers which represent the average fluctuation in stocks for a series of years, are facts which point in the direction of equilibrium, and well serve to show the constantly increasing solidity of American institutions. That tendency in the iron market to fluctuate between points less removed from each other is a fact of like implication, and that the emigration of persons will at some far distant day equal the immigration we must admit. This tendency to equilibrium is, however, not constant ; that is, it does not decrease from year to year with regularity, but is made up of rhythmical movements, which, taken as a whole, decrease from period to period, until at last they will end in comparative rest. Upon this point Mr. Spencer says : —

"It is observable that advance in organization, as well as advance in growth, is conducive to a better equilibrium of industrial functions. While the diffusion of mercantile information is slow, and the means of transport deficient, the adjustment of supply to demand is extremely imperfect ; great over-production of each commodity, followed by great under-production, constitute a rhythm having extremes that depart very widely from the mean state in which demand and supply are equilibrated. But when good roads are made, and there is a rapid diffusion of printed or written intelligence, and still more when railways and telegraphs come into existence ; when the periodical fairs of early days lapse into weekly markets and those into daily markets, — there is gradually produced a better balance of production and consumption ; extra demand is much more quickly followed by augmented supply ; and the rapid oscillations of price within narrow limits upon either side of a comparatively uniform mean indicate a near approach to equilibrium. Evidently this industrial progress has for its limit that which Mr. Mill has called the 'stationary state,' when population shall have become dense over all habitable parts of the globe; when the resources of every region have been fully explored; and when the productive arts admit of no further improvements; there must result an almost complete balance both between the fertility and mortality of each society, and between its producing and consuming activities. Each society will exhibit only minor deviations from its average number, and the rhythm of its industrial functions will go on from day to day, and year to year, with comparatively insignificant perturbations. This limit, however, though we are inevitably advancing towards it, is indefinitely remote; and can never, indeed, be absolutely reached. The peopling of the earth up to the point supposed cannot take place by simple spreading. In the future, as in the past, the process will be carried on rhythmically by waves of migration from new and higher centres of civilization successively arising; and by the supplanting of inferior races by the superior races they beget; and the process so carried on must be extremely slow."

Whether commercial rhythms are lengthened in time, and weakened in intensity, or whether they are both shortened in time and weakened in intensity, we are at present not prepared to say. We, at least, *do* know that the tendency of all prices is to fluctuate between lesser and lesser limits, and that the periods of commercial depression are not attended with as great sufferings as in former years. The shortening or lengthening in time, to which commercial waves are subject by reason of a loss of contained forces, is so insignificant, and the time before which such shortening will show any visible effect so remote, that it need not enter into the deliberations of business men whatever. The absolute or even the approximate equilibration of prices can take place only in an ideal society, and such a state will probably never be reached.

Though the reasoning contained in this chapter may not at present result in any practical good, still it is necessary for the symmetry of the argument that such observations should be made. The armentarium of a progressive science must include not alone a history of its past facts, but also its future possibilities. This chapter, however, becomes interesting and instructive to us when we observe the manner in which, as time goes on, the mutual advantages of the citizens of a community become still more and more intertwined, and how the interests of races are constantly growing more harmonious, until they shall eventually end in identity; and lastly, how absolutely and helplessly dependent are all races and peoples on those physical forces of which they form but an infinitesimal part.

CHAPTER X.

SUMMARY AND CONCLUSION.

It is now necessary that we should examine as a whole that which before we have only examined in parts. It remains for us to point out how each division fits each other part, the whole constituting an organized body of truth, in which resides the science we seek. Beginning with the chapters contained in Part First, we saw that the movements going on in the external world present to the mind the display of forces. Upon examination of these forces, we determined that the weaker would be always overcome by the stronger, and this conclusion, with certain modifying clauses, we imbedded in the proposition which has been called the Law of the Direction of Motion. Further study and comparison of natural phenomena taught us that though the first proposition which we had here formulated fully expressed the direction which each body would take from moment to moment, it did not express the character of that movement, and to the first proposition we added another, that expressed in a fuller sense the movements to which all phenomena are subject. This has been called the Law of Rhythm. With these two truths so deduced, we entered upon the study of general commercial affairs. We here found not only that the movements going on in all processes of exchange were in the line of least resistance, but also were composed of rhythms, small within larger; and we also found that the larger rhythms were completed only in the course of years.

We next examined the history of the iron industry. We found that the price and production of iron undergoes a continual ebb and flow, and we also noticed that the highest and lowest prices of iron were separated from each other by periods of from eight to ten years; and we also observed that when the price of iron was the highest, failures were the least numerous, and that they were the most numerous when the price was the least. Turning from this subject, we saw that the increase in the railroad mileage of the country was not a continuous ratio, but consisted of rhythms, the largest number of miles being built when the price of iron was the highest, and general business was in good condition, and the least number of miles when iron was the lowest, and the general business of the country was in poor condition. The table of the consumption of iron and steel rails agreed with the increase and decrease of railroad mileage.

We then examined the table which represents the number of persons who arrive each year from foreign countries, and we found, of the vast number of immigrants who have come to this country, the most have come in times of commercial activity, and the fewest in times of commercial depression.

The prices of stocks sold in the New York Stock Exchange, when reduced to a table where they can be compared, showed us that the periods of highest priced and best business years were separated from each other by intervals of about nine years, and that these high-priced years were the times in which, as our table of failures points out, generally business was most prosperous.

Examining next the figures which represent the yearly clearings of the New York banks, and which, moreover, represent in a certain degree the *domestic* trade of the country, and afterwards examining the figures furnished by the government Reports of imports and exports, which, being added together, fairly represent the total *foreign* trade of the country; we see that both the foreign and the domestic trade increase in amount as failures grow few and iron rises in price, and decrease in amount when failures again become relatively numerous and iron falls in price.

Thus far in our survey we observe that the commercial rhythms of which we have been treating, undergo a continual rise and fall. The lowest points at which iron is sold; the time at which the least number of immigrants arrive in the country; the time when railroad building is the least active; the time when stocks reach their lowest points; the time when failures are the most numerous; these times, with but minor difference, occur together. Similarly, when iron is high, failures are few; when stocks advance, railroad building and immigration increase. When one advances, they all advance. When one decreases, they all decrease. The general character of all tallies with the general character of each.[1]

These commercial rhythms not only agree with each other, but they complete themselves in approximately equal times. Thus in our study of the general business of the country, we saw that failures were least numerous, — and liabilities were the least, in periods ranging from eight to ten years. In reviewing the history of the iron trade we saw that the price of pig iron reached a high figure every eight or ten years. The history of the stock market acquainted us with like facts, and immigration and railroad building grows active or slow in about the same time.

In the chapter on Grain we saw that those forces which cause large and small crops are those over which man has no control, and the method of whose action he does not, as yet, fully understand. We moreover determined that the crop of cereals could not be the cause of those immense undulations which we have noticed in the commercial world, the record showing a larger crop per acre in the years of poor business, than in the years of good business, and so we can here simplify matters and eliminate that factor.

From the remainder of our evidence what conclusion shall we draw? What is the implication of the facts of which we here have a consensus? Will these ebbs and flows of commerce continue? What is to be their final out-

---

[1] See frontispiece.

come? The answer to the latter question has been foreshadowed in the chapter on Equilibration. That they will continue we cannot doubt. That these commercial movements, rising and falling through the centuries, are now to be brought to a sudden and complete standstill, even the most credulous would hardly dare assert. Future rhythms must, of course, be subject to the influences enumerated in the chapter on Equilibration; but, as we there decided, those influences are so slight as not to determine our immediate action, and we can therefore treat them as though they were not.

It is characteristic of every science that the laws which that science formulates are capable of proof by direct appeal to nature. The chemist who tells you that, when blue litmus paper is immersed in an acid solution, it will turn red, is held to have established his point if, upon going through the operation before your eyes, the results which he predicts are the results which you observe. The student of astronomy who tells you that the planet Jupiter will in six months pass a given point in the heavens, from which it is now far distant, is held to have a knowledge of the laws which regulate the movements of the heavenly bodies if, at the appointed time, the planet has reached the designated place. If, however, the astronomer fails to foretell *exactly* the time when the planet will cross that spot in the heavens before agreed upon, and misses by one, ten, or twenty minutes its time of passage, he is held to have established his point *provisionally;* the error between predicted and actual passage not being the result of any waywardness of Nature, but rather arising from the fact that his calculations have not included allowances for those minor disturbing forces, such as, for instance, the attractive force of some more distant planet, he being as yet unacquainted with its size, distance, and position. Similarly, the meteorologist who studies the phenomena of rains, calms, and storms could, had he the necessary data, foretell with exactness the approach of these atmospheric states. As it is, however, who shall decry the reports of the United States Signal Service because they are not in every instance absolutely correct. Who shall say that information concerning the approach of a storm has no value whatever to the owners of vessels?

The fact that a large and increasing percentage of weather forecasts are correct is held by all to be a conclusive proof that the time and money spent in collecting and arranging weather reports is not wasted. The method of proof taught us by the chemist, the astronomer, the meteorologist, has here a direct application. Theories are valueless unless they will work, and so it becomes our part to place these generalizations of business phenomena on record, and test their validity in exactly the same manner as other scientific generalizations are tested. With a wider knowledge may come a different interpretation, an interpretation in some degree opposed to that which we have given; but, all things considered, we may trust that we are at present not far wrong.

We have so far decided that commercial movements are in the line of least resistance; that they are rhythmic; that these rhythms complete themselves in approximately equal times, and that such will be their course in the future. Knowing these facts enables us to tell with approximate accuracy the course of commercial movements in years to come. Thus the history of the record of failures points to the year 1887 as being a time when, in proportion to the number engaged in business, failures will be most numerous. The history of the record of prices and consumption of pig iron points to the year 1886 or 1887 as the year when the average yearly price will reach its lowest point. The history of the record of railroad building, immigration and the New York Stock Market points to the same conclusion. Not that the downward grade of prices and of business will continue to go from bad to worse; even in this downward movement there is a rhythm of which we must take account. Some years will present a better showing than others, but that any genuine upward movement, lasting for three or four years, can begin before that time, we have no valid reason to believe. The upward movements in commerce, as we have learned, do not last less than two, or more than four years. The following remarks must be taken in the light of probabilities only, and are the natural results to which our course of reasoning has led.

1885.—This year business will probably be slightly better than in 1884, as a temporary reaction may take place, wing to the unprecedented declines of the year 1884. Failures over 11,000.

1886. — A great number of failures among small dealers, with capital of five thousand and under. Stocks lower. Wages lower.

1887. — A continuation of the history of 1886 for the greater part of this year. Stocks will begin to slowly advance. Iron about stationary, with a firm tendency. Failures among small traders will continue. Toward the close of the year prospects brighten.

1888. — During this year every department of business will have reached and passed its lowest point, and the advance will be well started.

1889. — Business of all kinds active and on the advance. Bright hopes for the future. Failures fewer. Stocks and iron higher. Wages higher. Immigration increasing. A great business boom.

1890. — Speculation rampant. Immigration large. Business continues good. Wages high. Iron and stocks reach their highest point and turn downward. Failures few.

1891. — During this year a conservative business course is advised. Though wages are high and failures comparatively few, keep prepared for financial storms. The inflation of prices, the increase of activity, will not last forever, During and after the year 1891 look out for breakers ahead.

Such appears to be a fair view of the conditions we may

expect to encounter during the next seven years. During the years of depression into which we are now entering, — 1885, 1886, 1887, — we may expect numerous strikes, mobs, and troubles in our cities among laboring classes, incident to such times. There will also be revivals in religion during those years; for it has been noticed that at such times — whether because they have nothing else to do, or because they feel their own weakness — men are prone to call upon a Higher Power for consolation and aid. It may be objected to by some, that, while it is evident that commercial movements are regularly recurrent, we, as yet, are not sufficiently acquainted with their periodicity to be able to extend those movements into the future. It is replied, that we have an undoubted right to judge from what we know, and it is better to form some idea of coming events from that knowledge, than to pusillanimously cast such knowledge aside, and unreservedly give ourselves up to circumstances. If we accept the teachings of the — to us — minor facts of nature as being reliable guides of conduct, we must also accept her major teachings. Between accepting knowledge at all, and knowledge in its entirety, there is no choice, provided always that such knowledge is well founded. The predictions here marked out may not in their minor points be absolutely correct, but he who will give the evidence upon which they are based a careful and impartial study will find that in their general character they faithfully represent the *a priori* probabilities.

Have we any other means of judging of the future than

by the past? Let any one who doubts the conclusions here reached, and thinks he can furnish a better course, put on his thinking-cap, call to activity his proudest reasoning powers, follow any course of thought but that there contained, and see how widely he will miss the mark. If the lessons which we learn from the collection and arrangement of statistics are not to be of some value to us, we had best discontinue the expense and labor of their collection.

These truths, drawn from a wide class of business facts, are of value to each business man. The wholesale dealer, who has on hand a large stock of goods bought at constantly increasing prices, must see to it that, at the turn of affairs, he is not left with a supply on his hands for which there is no call, and on which he will be obliged to sacrifice. The retail dealer, who invests his savings in a store, and stocks it with such articles as the laborers need, must, if he lives in a town whose principal industry is the iron trade, time his affairs to the fluctuations of that business. The speculator who, in the assurance born of ignorance, endeavors to bull the stock market during the years of depression, will see his profits melt slowly away; and even a rising market, the wise must remember, will not last forever. The manufacturer must intelligently foresee the trend of future events, or suffer the consequences of his ignorance. The clerk, the lawyer, the doctor, and even the clergyman, are affected, both in their salaries and their fees, by the course of the business world. In fact, there is no class of society, and no man in the country, who is not, to some extent, influenced by these periodical fluctuations which we have been considering. They are then, indeed, worthy of our study; and that knowledge which we thereby gain, if acted up to by all, will hasten that complete equilibration, bringing with it the greatest happiness and the most enlightened society.

As to the causes of these regularly recurring commercial movements, many theories have been put forward. Some have considered business depressions as due to a general over-production of commodities. Others say that this view is absurd; that there can never be too much corn, or clothing, or boots and shoes, or any other commodity. We can imagine one of those who would explain business depressions as the direct result of an excess of supply, when replying to the iron worker who asks for work in order that he may buy bread, as saying, "Very well, stop producing and you will get it;" who, to the maker of boots and shoes who says, "I wish to exchange my goods for clothing," replies, "Very well, don't make so many boots and shoes, and the clothing will be forthcoming." In effect he says, "If you want to obtain the satisfaction of your desires, stop work, do not try to get what you want." A contradiction is here involved. We may observe the fallacy of this position by going through the following brief argument.

What constitutes the means of payment for commodities? It is simply commodities. Each person's means of payment lies in what he produces; therefore, the more he produces, the more he can buy. A general over-production of commodities above the demand, as far as demand consists in the means of payment, is, according to this view, impossible. On the other hand, some say it may not be the ability to purchase, but the desire to possess, which falls short, and so more things come to be offered for sale than the people, as a whole, desire to have. That is to say, there is a limit to human desires. This view is conceivable, but the fact that each citizen goes on producing and striving to fill his desires at all seasons and all times, proves that this is not actually the case. So far as we know man, there never can be a falling off in demand because of a satiety of all his desires.

While there can never be a general lack of desire to possess, or a general over-supply of commodities, yet the demand may, in some cases, be for one thing, and the supply of another; in which event, production may be said to be not excessive, but ill-assorted. For instance, a blacksmith may go among a community of woodsmen who are well supplied with axes, and, thinking that woodsmen certainly need axes, he may make a large number and endeavor to sell them, He finds that, every one being supplied, there is no sale for his goods, and in this case there is an overproduction, not of all things, but of one thing. The woodsmen want something, — the fact that they put forth efforts proves this; they may want flour, and the blacksmith has produced axes, in which case production may be said to be ill-assorted, but not excessive.

On the same principle there is, in a commercial crisis, an excess of all commodities above the *money* demand; in other words, an under supply of money. Production is not excessive, but ill-assorted as concerns the money demand.

From the sudden annihilation of a large mass of credit, every one dislikes to part with ready money, and every one desires to obtain it. There is a general rush to sell, and prices fall, not becauses demand ceases, but because money is scarce.

"But it is a great error to suppose with Sismondi," says Mr. Mill, from whose work on Political Economy a portion of the foregoing is culled, "that a commercial crisis is the effect of a general excess of production. It is simply the consequence of an excess of speculative purchases. Its immediate cause is a contraction of credit, and the remedy is, not a diminution of supply, but a restoration of confidence." Now, the ability of a purchaser is made of three things, — money, property, and credit: as the sum of these three is large or small, in that proportion can a buyer purchase.

If it be conceded that there never can be an over-production of commodities, and that there never can be a lack of desire to acquire commodities; and if it be further conceded that a general rise of prices is caused — as political economists say it is caused — by everybody buying to the extent of their ability because there is a general impression that prices will rise or ought to rise; and that a general fall of prices, or crisis, is caused by everybody selling because there is a general impression that prices are about to fall, still we are no forwarder than before in understanding the phenomena. Whence the *general impression* that has caused the rise and afterwards the fall? Why should these *general impressions* occur in different countries at the same time, and why should they occur in about equal periods, are questions that naturally arise, and for which there are no satisfactory answers.

Some think that the phenomena we are here considering are due to changes in fashion, meaning by the word "fashion" the constant differentiation of wants and desires of men that is noticeable in a progressive society, and that the only way to avoid the evils which attend times of depression is to cultivate foresight by studying as accurately as possible the nature of human desires and the changes that have been observed to take place in them. Truly a difficult task, if one is not furnished with some organizing principle by which human desires are explicable. To say that business sagacity, the ability to foresee the trend of events, can only be acquired by the study of human desires, is to say that from the study of this swaying, swirling, ever-changing, tumultous sea of life one is to catch the salient features of this involved and kaleidoscopic interchange of wants, cravings, and yearnings, and from them to decide his actions, — to start with such a supposition would land the investigator either in infinities or in the insane asylum. The number of human desires is so great, and the variety so complex, that to strive to unravel the tangled mass would be more than finite wisdom can accomplish.

Some suppose that low profits cause all the trouble, and that nothing needs to be done but "regulate" competition, and then all commercial troubles would cease to exist. If this explanation be received and acted upon, society would revert to the purely militant type, such as, for instance, was that of the people who built the pyramids. It would be necessary that there should be one great regulator, and a host of overseers, and overseers of overseers, to see to it that his commands were obeyed and the delinquents punished.[1]

Politicians, reading history and bringing away from it the names of a few great men and the stories of "decisive" battles, tacitly admit that these men and their actions made that history when they assume that the policy of political parties is the true cause of commercial distress,— policies, it must be remembered, the majority of which history has universally stamped as wrong, and which new generations require to constantly make over.

Some, the late Professor Jevons for instance, consider that panics are caused by the coming and going of the sun-spots; these affecting the crops, and through the crops

---

[1] This is the position taken by one branch of the Socialistic Labor Party, who propose that the government should own all land, railroads, telegraph and telephone lines, that it should "regulate" all freight and passenger rates, telegraph and telephone tolls, rents, hours of labor, wages of laborers, profits on capital, etc.

affecting the rise and fall of prices; others think that large or small crops have very little influence on the commercial world at large, the difference between the amounts of large and small crops being insignificant when compared to the difference between prices in active and slow times.

Some would refer all commercial troubles to the policy of the banks. Concerning the panic of 1873 it was testified that "their capital needed for legitimate purposes was practically lent out on certain iron rails, railroad ties, bridges, and rolling-stock *called* railroads, many of them laid down in places where these materials were practically useless." No one, as yet, however, has pointed out the reason why the banks have not as good a right to loan their capital on railroads as on personal notes, real estate, or any other kind of security.

It is a fact which most business men will not deny, that banks do not loan money unless they have a pretty certain belief that they will get it back. The fact that the property which to-day is of ample value to secure the loan becomes of little or no value to-morrow is not the fault of the banks, but rather lies in the circumstances of the property.

Some think that the operations of the large stock speculators make "good" or "bad" times. If the gentlemen of the New York Stock Exchange who managed the recent attempt to "peg up" prices would step forward and explain their success, those who entertain this idea would probably be answered.

Others believe that a commercial crisis can be readily explained as the result of over-immigration,—a plethora of laborers all consuming more than can with facility be produced. Others think that a too rapid increase of population would generate, as fast as it would become unbalanced, a retarding effect, and that this is the explanation. Some think that the planet Jupiter exercises an influence on prices, and, like Wallenstein's astrologer, would read the destiny of commerce in the horoscope of the stars.

Concerning all which opinions, all that can be said is, that no one can be entirely right, neither can each be entirely wrong. Each opinion possibly contains some truth, nor yet would a consensus of all opinions represent the full truth. When it is understood (and there are signs that it will be) that society is a growth, that the civilization of the present day is the product of all civilizations that have gone before, and is the parent of the civilization that is to come; when it is understood that this growth goes on under the influence of laws not capricious and fanciful, but as certain and sure in action as is the operation of that force by which a stone is drawn to the earth; when it is understood that society, having its roots imbedded in the savage life of far-off ages, has been and is slowly coming to its blossom; when it is understood that hereafter it will be through these rhythmical movements of prices that commercial equilibration will be established, and so a social equilibration; then it will be seen that these phenomena, terrible as are their effects upon some, are the natural and necessary parts of one unfolding plan.

In some manner, — it is not as yet known in what manner, — these commercial movements play a most important part in the development of the race. If it is true that they exhibit such a tendency as was pointed out in the chapter on Equilibration, then they can never cease until the race is fully developed, — that is to say, until individual character becomes perfect, — and this state manifestly can only be approximately reached.

Moreover no such arrangement of society as that contemplated by the Socialists can attain to this result. The division of property and labor equally between all members of a society cannot permanently take place until each member deserves it. The strong mind in the strong body must have the benefit of his superiority. The evil mind in the evil body must suffer the consequences of his inferiority. The wise cannot sink to the level of the ignorant. The ignorant must rise to the level of the wise. This has hitherto been the rule, and will in all probability henceforth be the rule.

Any attempt to substitute the power of the state for the power of the individual beyond certain limits is little better than despotism; and despotism or socialism once accomplished, a revolution is necessary to again establish society upon its natural basis. Social equilibration has gone on *pari passu* with the equilibration of prices, and these with the improvement of average character, and, as far as we know, there is no hope that one will be equilibrated before the other. If we admit that business motions are in the line of least resistance, and rhythmic, and that these rhythms show a tendency to become balanced, we may conclude that panics and periods of depression will always continue at intervals, with this qualification, — the next period of depression will not be as severe as the present, and the next less severe, and so on, until, to all outward signs, they will at last cease.

A business man, in order to be successful, must take into account these progressive changes going on in the commercial world, and, as we would disapprove the conduct of that sailor who puts to sea in time of storm, with leaky boat and without a compass, so we should disapprove the conduct of that business man who enters commercial life amid dangers as great, and without any detailed plan of manœuvre. Indeed, when it is known that only a paltry four or five out of every hundred engaged in active business attain, in a lifetime, to a permanent and profitable competency, the attractions which it presents are difficult to understand.

Statistics, though often dry and uninteresting, if carefully collected and properly presented, are among the greatest aids to commercial success. They are to business men what the mile-post is to the traveller, and the magnetic needle to the seaman — unerring guides across the financial seas. They are indispensable to modern civilization, and a proper study of them presents to us facts of deep importance and of incalculable worth. The labor of compiling statistics is often a thankless task ; but if, when brought together and compared, they show a system of commercial movements, such as we have been considering, and which enables us to lift for a moment the veil of the future, should we not accord the highest praise to those men whose honest and long-continued efforts have made such knowledge possible!

And now, retiring a space, and looking back over our course from a point where details are lost to view, we see that our study, in its general character and in the conclu sions we have drawn from it, is indeed worthy the name of science. When so viewed, it presents to the mind a mode of action in commercial affairs with which we before were not familiar, and of which we had only dreamed. What the poet said, probably in fancy, long ago in the days of Queen Elizabeth, is to-day an indisputable fact. There *is* a tide in the affairs of men. His conception of the course of affairs, however, becomes dwarfed beside that which we of a later age, with the positive knowledge which science furnishes, are enabled to form. When we look back over the majestic march of civilization, and behold these vast commercial waves, bearing upon their bosoms the fate of men and of nations, now raising their crests to the heavens, and again plunging into the abyss ; and when, from the vantage ground of our little Present, we look forward into the Future, and behold how by their own inherent forces they will at last be stilled, — the understanding becomes aware of a purpose as vast, and of a method of action as perfect, as is any other manifestation of the workings of that Unknowable Power of which everything in Nature, yea Nature herself, is but the efflux and the sequence.

PENDING ISSUES.

Economic and Political Science.

Atkinson. The Distribution of Products; or, the Mechanism and the Metaphysics of Exchange. Three Essays. What Makes the Rate of Wages? What is a Bank? The Railway, the Farmer, and the Public. By EDWARD ATKINSON. Second edition, revised and enlarged, with new statistical material. 8vo, cloth . . $1 50

"It would be difficult to mention another book that gives so effective a presentation of the present conditions and methods of industry, and of the marvels that have been wrought in the arts of production and transportation during the past fifty years."—*Advertiser*, Boston.

Cossa. Taxation, Its Principles and Methods. A Translation of the "First Principles of the Science of Finance." By Professor LUIGI COSSA, Ph.D., of the University of Pavia. Edited with notes by HORACE WHITE 1 00

Moore. Friendly Sermons to Protectionists and Manufacturers. By J. S. MOORE. (Economic Monograph, No. 4) . . 25

O'Neil. The American Electoral System. An Analysis of Its Character and Its History. By CHARLES A. O'NEIL, of the New York Bar. 12mo, ... 1 50

"The author's plans and compilations will be found valuable, and the book is well worth having and studying."—*Ohio State Journal*.

"We hail as hopeful the appearance of any thoughtful work on this vital subject, Mr. O'Neil has given us a timely and valuable book."—*Public Opinion*, Washington.

"Mr. O'Neil's book is full of valuable suggestions, and deserves a careful reading by all who are interested in our political system."—*Boston Traveller*.

Schoenhof. The Industrial Situation and the Question of Wages. A Study in Social Physiology. By J. SCHOENHOF, author of "The Destructive Influence of the Tariff," etc. (Questions of the Day Series, No. XXX.) 8vo, cloth 1 00

—— **The Destructive Influence of the Tariff upon Manufacture and Commerce, and the Facts and Figures Relating Thereto.** By J. SCHOENHOF. (Questions of the Day Series, No. IX.) 8vo, cloth, 75 cents; paper 40

"An able presentation of the subject by a practical man, which should have a wide circulation."

G. P. PUTNAM'S SONS, NEW YORK AND LONDON

Sumner. Lectures on the History of Protection in the United States. By Prof. W. G. SUMNER, of Yale College. 8vo, cloth extra 75

"There is nothing in the literature of free trade more forcible and effective than this little book."—*N. Y. Evening Post.*

Sterne. The Constitutional History and Political Development of the United States. An Analytical Study. By SIMON STERNE, of the New York Bar. Second edition, revised with editions. 12mo, cloth 1 25

Taussig. The Tariff History of the United States, 1789-1888. Comprising the material contained in "Protection to Young Industries" and "History of the Present Tariff," together with the revisions and additions needed to complete the narrative. By Prof. F. W. TAUSSIG. 12mo, cloth. (Questions of the Day Series, No. XLVII.) 1 25

"Tracts like this will be read by many who would not open a bulky volume of the same title, and they will find that what they regarded as the most confused and perplexing of subjects is not only comprehensible, but also interesting."—*The Nation.*

The President's Message. With Annotations of Facts and Figures. By R. R. BOWKER. (Questions of the Day Series, No. XLIX.) 25

A republication, in convenient form for reference, of the clear and business-like statement made by President Cleveland, in his latest message to Congress, of the economical issues now before the country for decision.

Wells. Practical Economics. A collection of Essays respecting certain of the Economic Experiences of the United States. By DAVID A. WELLS. 8vo, cloth 1 50

CHIEF CONTENTS.—A Modern Financial Utopia—The True Story of the Leaden Images—The Taxation of Distilled Spirits—Recent Phases of the Tariff Question—Tariff Revision—The Pauper-Labor Argument—The Silver Question—Measures of Value—The Production and Distribution of Wealth.

—— **Our Merchant Marine.** How it Rose, Increased, became Great, Declined and Decayed. By DAVID A. WELLS. (Questions of the Day Series, No. III.)

—— **Why We Trade and How We Trade,** or an enquiry into the extent to which the existing commercial and fiscal policy of the United States restricts the material prosperity and development of the country. By DAVID A. WELLS. (Economic Monograph, No. 1) . 25

G. P. PUTNAM'S SONS, NEW YORK AND LONDON

RECENT
Political and Economic Publications.

WELLS (David A., LL.D., D.C.L.). **Practical Economics.** A Series of Essays Respecting Certain of the Recent Economic Experiences of the United States. Octavo, pp. vi. + 259 . $1 50

> "Few writers are more thoroughly studied by economists, or more worthy of study, and it long ago ceased to be necessary to speak of any thing from his hands as 'valuable' and 'worthy of attention.'"—*Literary World*, Boston.
>
> "They present in permanent form a mass of information about the actual working of the protective system which nobody but Mr. Wells possesses."—*N. Y. Times*.

—— **Our Merchant Marine.** How it rose, increased, became great, declined, and decayed; with an enquiry into the conditions essential to its resuscitation and prosperity. Octavo, cloth, $1 00

> "Ought to be studied carefully by all intelligent citizens."—*Congregationalist*.
>
> "Full to the brim of facts."—*Standard*, Syracuse.
>
> "Cannot be brought too prominently before the public."—*Argus*, Albany.

—— **Why We Trade and How We Trade**; or, An Enquiry into the Extent to which the Existing Commercial and Fiscal Policy of the United States Restricts the Material Prosperity and Development of the Country. Octavo, paper . . . $0 25

> "It is a good sign of the times when such pamphlets, by able writers, are published in cheap form, so as to be accessible to all."—*Baltimore Gazette*.

TAUSSIG (Prof. F. W.). **The Tariff History of the United States—1789-1888.** Comprising the material contained in "Protection to Young Industries" and "History of the Present Tariff," together with revisions and additions needed to complete the narrative. 12mo, cloth $1 25

> "At a time when the tariff has come to occupy the forefront among political questions, we can heartily commend this book to all political enquirers."—*Post*, Washington.
>
> "Can be recommended to those wishing to arrive at a comprehensive understanding of the tariff system, as the best work of the day."—*Boston Times*.

G. P. PUTNAM'S SONS, NEW YORK AND LONDON.

RECENT
Political and Economic Publications.

SUMNER (Prof. W. G.). **Lectures on the History of Protection in the United States.** Octavo . . . $0 75

"There is nothing in the literature of free trade more forcible and effective than this little book."—*N. Y. Evening Post.*

SCHOENHOF (J.). **The Destructive Influence of the Tariff upon Manufacture and Commerce,** and the Facts and Figures Relating thereto. Octavo, cloth $0 75

"As an argument it is absolutely conclusive."—*Literary Churchman.*

"We recommend the book to all who are interested in this great question of the day."—*The News and Courier*, Charleston.

MOORE (J. S.). **Friendly Sermons to Protectionists and Manufacturers.** Octavo, paper . . $0 25

——— **Friendly Letters to American Farmers and Others.** Octavo, paper $0 25

BASTIAT (Frederic). **Sophisms of Protection.** With Preface by Horace White. 12mo $1 00

"The most telling statements of the leading principles of the free-trade theory ever published."—*The Nation.*

——— **Essays on Political Economy.** 12mo . . $1 25

"The laws of an abstruse science have never been made more clear, or expressed more forcibly "—*Cincinnati Commercial.*

ROOSEVELT (Hon. Theodore). **Essays on Practical Politics.** Octavo, cloth $0 75

STERNE (Simon). **The Constitutional History and Political Development of the United States.** Second edition, revised with additions $1 25

"An able and instructive résumé of the political history of the country. . . . A book which every American should read. . . . Contains just the data needed by the voter."—*Rutland Standard.*

G. P. PUTNAM'S SONS, New York and London.

www.ingramcontent.com/pod-product-compliance
Lightning Source LLC
Chambersburg PA
CBHW032138160426
43197CB00008B/695